W9-ADS-002

PRESENTING

Phyllis Reynolds Naylor

Twayne's United States Authors Series
Young Adult Authors

Patricia J. Campbell, General Editor

TUSAS 676

PHYLLIS REYNOLDS NAYLOR

Cover artwork of some of her books hangs on the wall of her family room. *Photo courtesy of the National Education Association, taken by Carolyn Salisbury.*

PRESENTING

Phyllis Reynolds Naylor

Lois Thomas Stover

St. Mary's College of Maryland

Twayne Publishers
An Imprint of Simon & Schuster Macmillan
New York

Prentice Hall International
London Mexico City New Delhi Singapore Sydney Toronto

Twayne's United States Authors Series No. 676

Presenting Phyllis Reynolds Naylor
Lois Thomas Stover

Copyright © 1997 by Twayne Publishers

Twayne Publishers
An Imprint of Simon & Schuster Macmillan
1633 Broadway
New York, NY 10019–6785

Library of Congress Cataloging-in-Publication Data

Stover, Lois T.
　　Presenting Phyllis Reynolds Naylor / Lois Thomas Stover.
　　　　p.　cm. — (Twayne's United States authors series : TUSAS 676
　Young adult authors)
　　　　Summary: Examines the major works of the author of the Newbery Award-winning "Shiloh," provides biographical background, and discusses some of the efforts to censor her work.
　　　　ISBN 0-8057-7805-5 (alk. paper)
　　　　1. Naylor, Phyllis Reynolds—Criticism and interpretation.
　　2. Young adult fiction, American—History and criticism.
　　[1. Naylor, Phyllis Reynolds—Criticism and interpretation.
　　2. American literature—History and criticism.]　I. Title.
　　II. Series: Twayne's United States authors series ; TUSAS 676.
　　III. Series: Twayne's Unites States authors series.　Young adult
　　authors.
　PS3564.A9Z87　1997
　　813'.54—DC20　　　　　　　　　　　　　　　　　　　96-36022
　　　　　　　　　　　　　　　　　　　　　　　　　　　　　　CIP
　　　　　　　　　　　　　　　　　　　　　　　　　　　　　　AC

10 9 8 7 6 5 4 3 2 1

Printed in the United States of America

For my wonderful family

(With special thanks to Patty Campbell and Phyllis Reynolds Naylor for their patience, encouragement, and support throughout the work on this project.)

Contents

Foreword

The advent of Twayne's Young Adult Author Series in 1985 was a response to the growing stature and value of adolescent literature and the lack of serious critical evaluation of the new genre. The first volume in the series was heralded as marking the coming-of-age of young adult fiction.

The aim of the series is twofold. First, it enables young readers to research the work of their favorite authors and to see them as real people. Each volume is written in a lively, readable style and attempts to present in an attractive, accessible format a vivid portrait of the author as a person.

Second, the series provides teachers and librarians with insights and background material for promoting and teaching young adult novels. Each of the biocritical studies is a serious literary analysis of one author's work (or one subgenre within young adult literature), with attention to plot structure, theme, character, setting, and imagery. In addition, many of the series writers delve deeper into the creative writing process by tracking down early drafts or unpublished manuscripts by their subject authors, consulting with their editors or other mentors, and examining influences from literature, film, or social movements.

Many of the contributing authors of the series are among the leading scholars and critics of adolescent literature. Some are even YA novelists themselves. Each study is based on extensive interviews with the subject author and an exhaustive study of his or her work. Although the general format is the same, the individual volumes are uniquely shaped by their subjects, and each brings a different perspective to the classroom.

The goal of the series is to produce a succinct but comprehensive study of the life and art of every leading YA writer, as well as to trace how that art has been accepted by readers and critics, and to evaluate its place in the developing field of adolescent literature. And—perhaps most important—to inspire a reading and rereading of this quality fiction that speaks so directly to young people about their life experiences.

PATRICIA J. CAMPBELL, General Editor

Preface

I read my first Phyllis Reynolds Naylor title when I was a young adult. I was working at the local public library shelving books after school and reading whatever looked interesting that crossed my path during slack times. I remember, as a junior in high school, gobbling up *No Easy Circle* in one sitting. I was fascinated by Naylor's description of the counterculture that was so much a part of the late sixties and early seventies and intrigued by the main character's efforts to make peace with herself as she grows apart from her best friend—something my friends and I were experiencing. Later, when I became a junior high teacher, my students introduced me to Naylor's "Alice" books, and a friend pursuing her doctorate in clinical psychology told me to read *Crazy Love: An Autobiographical Account of Marriage and Madness* after a professor had assigned it for a course she was taking. I was in awe of Naylor's honesty and her skill in sharing exactly what she felt and experienced when dealing with a very ill husband.

My love of Naylor's work has always been that of a reader for a writer who makes her cry and laugh and thus feel better able to face the world. I was fortunate to be able to meet the woman whose books I have so appreciated when we met for lunch and an afternoon of conversation at King's Contrivance, a restaurant in Columbia, Maryland, on July 7, 1995. She arrived wearing a white peasant blouse and a full cotton skirt, her feet in sandals, and she carried a manuscript with her that she was in the process of copyediting; she clearly does not waste one precious minute of her day. She has a lovely smile, warm and welcoming—but her demeanor hides a strength of will that is found in many of her characters. She had made the reservations, asking specifically for a quiet spot. We found ourselves near an air-conditioning duct surrounded by other patrons engaged in animated conversation, and she politely, but very firmly, requested an alternative.

For several hours that day, Naylor told me about her life, her family, her passion for her work, her cats, her writing group, her home. Unless otherwise noted, quotations from the author came from that interview. Over the past year Naylor has graciously corresponded with me, continuing to answer my questions and sharing the details of her personal and professional life. The writer behind the books is able to create empathetic, insightful, interesting characters because she herself is an intelligent, passionate, articulate woman who cares deeply about both her craft and her various audiences. In *Presenting Phyllis Reynolds Naylor*, I hope to demonstrate more fully, in a systematic way, why she deserves a place of honor among those who write for young adults.

When Patty Campbell, the editor of Twayne's Young Adult Authors series, first mentioned to me the idea of doing a critical biography of Phyllis Reynolds Naylor, she told me that I would have to convince her that Naylor is, in fact, a young adult author. Campbell noted that Naylor has published a great deal for children, as well as for adults, and said, therefore, that she wanted to be certain that a book about Naylor belonged in the young adult author series.

After reading the almost eighty books Naylor has written, I believe that it is in her young adult titles that her writing gifts best find expression. Her compassion for the anxieties and very difficult decisions young adults face, coupled with her sense of humor, make her a favorite with this age group. She manages to provide a sense of comfort to her readers because she shows them other adolescents in tense situations who manage to survive and continue to mature, often because they, themselves, learn to relax, to enjoy who they are, to accept responsibility for the direction of their lives, and to see the humor in the world around them.

She takes herself seriously as a writer for young adults, as someone who understands the ways in which young people struggle to define themselves as their bodies change and their worlds expand, and as they recognize the fact that they have to take responsibility for their own destinies. Here, then, is Phyllis Reynolds Naylor.

Chronology

1933   Born in Anderson, Indiana, January 4. Middle child of Eugene Spencer Reynolds and Lura Mae (Schield) Reynolds.

1951   Graduates from high school; marries first husband.

1953   Receives diploma for associate's degree from Joliet Junior College, Joliet, Illinois.

1953–1956   Works as a clinical secretary for Billings Hospital, Chicago, Illinois.

1956   Serves as an elementary teacher in Hazelcrest, Illinois; first husband begins to show signs of severe mental illness.

1956–1959   Moves frequently, while writing for various Christian and commercial publications, in an effort to find appropriate care for first husband.

1958–1959   Serves as assistant executive secretary for the Montgomery County Education Association in Maryland.

1959–1960   Serves as Editorial Assistant for the *NEA Journal*, Washington, D.C.; divorces first husband.

1960   Marries Rex Vaughn Naylor; begins writing full-time.

1962   First son, Alan Jeffrey (Jeff), born.

1963   Graduates with a B.A. in Psychology from American University.

1965   First book, *The Galloping Goat and Other Stories*, published with Abingdon Press.

1966   Second son, Michael Scott, born.

1967   First novel, *What the Gulls Were Singing*, published with Follett.

1967   First young adult novel, *To Shake a Shadow*, published with Abingdon.

1971   *Wrestle the Mountain* honored as Junior Literary Guild selection.

1974–1975   Serves as President of the Children's Book Guild of Washington, D.C.

1975   First "Witch" book, *Witch's Sister*.

1976   *Walking through the Dark*, a novel for young adults, honored as a Junior Literary Guild selection.

1977   First adult book, *Crazy Love: An Autobiographical Account of Marriage and Madness*, honored as a Literary Guild Selection.

1978   *How I Came to Be a Writer* wins Golden Kite Award for nonfiction.

1982   *A String of Chances* selected by Young Adult Library Services Association of the American Library Association as a Best Book for Young Adults and as a Notable Trade Book in the Field of Social Studies by *Social Education*.

1983   *The Mad Gasser of Bessledorf Street*, first "Bessledorf" book, published.

1984   *A Triangle Has Four Sides*, a collection of young adult short stories, becomes her last publication with a Christian press.

1985   *Night Cry* wins Edgar Allen Poe Award for best juvenile mystery.

   The Dark of the Tunnel selected as a Notable Children's Trade Book in the Field of Social Studies by *Social Education*.

   The Agony of Alice, first "Alice" book.

1986   *The Keeper* chosen as a Junior Literary Guild Selection, selected as an ALA Notable and as YALSA Best Book for Young Adults.

   Unexpected Pleasures selected as a YALSA Best Book for Young Adults.

1987   *The Year of the Gopher* selected by YALSA as a Best Book for Young Adults, wins "Best YA Book of the Year" from Michigan Library Association.

1988   *Maudie in the Middle* wins International Book Award, Society of School Librarians.

1989   *Keeping a Christmas Secret*, picture book, wins Christopher Award.

   "My Dad Can't Be Crazy ... Can He?" adapted from *The Keeper* airs on September 14 on ABC as an *After-School Special*.

1991   *Shiloh* wins Newbery Award.

1991   *All But Alice* selected as a Notable Children's Book and as a Recommended Book for the Reluctant Reader by American Library Association/YALSA.

1993   *Alice in April* selected as a Recommended Book for the Reluctant Young Adult Reader by ALA/YALSA.

1. On Becoming and Staying a Writer

Phyllis Reynolds Naylor's body of work spans the spectrum of genres; she has written picture books, skits, short stories, nonfiction, autobiographical works, mysteries, time travel books, humorous books, and traditional young adult problem novels. In addition to being incredibly prolific, publishing 78 books between 1960 and 1995, Naylor is a consistently solid writer whose works have won much critical acclaim. The Newbery she received for *Shiloh* (1991) has been the highest of the many honors given to her work over time. Her books have been translated into numerous other languages, and *The Keeper* (1986) became an ABC *After-School Special* production entitled "My Dad Can't Be Crazy . . . Can He?" starring Loretta Swit.

What is the history of this gentle, soft-spoken woman with a passion for writing that seems only to grow stronger with the years? Phyllis Naylor, born in Anderson, Indiana, in 1933, was the younger daughter of Lura Mae (Schield), a sometime school teacher, and Eugene Spencer Reynolds, who worked in sales. Because of her father's line of work, the family frequently moved from town to town when Naylor was a young girl. In *How I Came to Be a Writer* (1978), Naylor describes those early years, reflecting on the nature of her family and on several significant aspects of her childhood that contributed to her development as a writer. Since her family found itself uprooted so often, Naylor derived a sense of home from shared family experiences. Family reading time and family trips to visit both sets of grandparents were two key elements in Naylor's childhood that have influenced her writing.

A Reader Becomes a Writer

Naylor describes the volumes of books in her childhood homes as "treasured friends," and she values the fact that her parents' abilities as readers drew her into the world of stories. Both her mother and father acted in plays during their time in college, and they used their thespian skills both to scare and delight their children. Naylor recalls, for instance, her mother's dramatic voice recounting the problems of the Israelites on their way to the Promised Land, and her father's ability to become different characters—from the deep-voiced Injun Joe to the high-pitched tones of Becky Thatcher in *Huckleberry Finn*—by changing his vocal quality. She still remembers those readings that had the power to make her, her older sister Norma, and her younger brother John shiver, such as James Whitcomb Riley's "Little Orphant Annie" with its scary refrain, "And the goblins'll get ya if ya don't watch out." Books such as *Egermeier's Bible Story Book*, two volumes of Grimm's fairy tales, the complete Mark Twain, *Collier's Encyclopedia*, and a collection of Sherlock Holmes stories kept her company throughout her childhood days. She even used them as props for make-believe plays. These same volumes would become building blocks or a stage for a puppet show, or would hold a bedsheet tent or curtain in place for an in-house theater. She writes,

> Even now, it bothers me to see, in someone's study, rows of pristine books that look as though they've never been opened, much less read and treasured—and certainly never used for holding bedsheets in place.[1]

By the time Naylor entered kindergarten, she was making up stories, imitating those she had heard so often at home. One of her very first efforts, for instance, was a story she dictated to her teacher that sounded remarkably like "The Juniper Tree" by the Brothers Grimm, a story that delighted her because of its gruesomeness. When she had not quite figured out the relationship between letters on the page and the words they formed, she would make up stories to accompany the pictures in her readers.[2] By fifth grade, Naylor found herself "on call" as the school's "writer in residence." She recalls, for example, being asked to give up her recess one day to generate, on the spur of the moment, a poem to celebrate the principal's birthday. During her free time at home, she wrote little books, using the backs of discarded paper; the children were not allowed to use clean paper for their writing and drawing, so Naylor would scour the wastepaper baskets for whatever she could find. She says,

> I would staple these sheets together and sometimes paste a strip of colored paper over the staples to give it the appearance of a bound book. Then I would grandly begin my story, writing the words at the top of each page and drawing an accompanying picture on the bottom. Sometimes I typed the story before stapling the pages. And sometimes I even cut old envelopes in half and pasted them on the inside covers as pockets, slipping an index card in each one, like a library book, so I could check it out to friends and neighbors. I was author, illustrator, printer, binder, and librarian all in one. (*How I Came*, 15–16)

Inspired by young Naylor's fascination with the detective Nancy Drew, these books were often about a character named Penny who solved mysteries. Because Naylor's sister, the artist in the family, had taught her how to draw lacy underwear, at some point during the story Penny would have to lose her clothes so that Naylor's newly developed illustrative skill could come into play! After her mother explained the facts of life to her, Naylor wrote *Manual for Pregnant Women*—with illustrations by the author—using her writing as a way to process this intriguing new knowledge. To this day, Naylor continues to collect information that fascinates her, storing newspaper clippings, magazine articles, and other material in file folders that she can refer to when appropriate.

The Naylor home, Bethesda, Maryland.

Family photo when Phyllis was 18. Back row: brother-in-law Jim Hinton, sister Norma, mother and father. Front row: dog Pepper, brother John, cat Sugar, and Naylor herself.

When she was 16, Naylor heard from a former Sunday school teacher who knew of her interest in writing. The teacher, who had become the editor of a Sunday school paper, suggested that Naylor write something for that paper. "Mike's Hero" was published in *Boys' and Girls' Comrade*. For this story, Naylor received her first check— in the sum of $4.67—in payment for a piece of writing. Looking back at that story now, Naylor describes it as too sentimental, as containing unrealistic dialogue and implausible plot events based around rather extraordinary coincidences. However, the teacher-turned-editor asked for more, and soon Naylor was publishing holiday poems, adventure/rescue stories, and many tales about bad children who learned their lessons and felt remorse.

For two years, Naylor tried to move out of the Sunday school market. She sent off stories to classic children's and young adult journals, from *Jack and Jill* to *Boy's Life* and *Seventeen*. They were returned with rejection slips. In *How I Came to Be a Writer*, Naylor describes how her dreams of fame as a writer vanished, replaced by a new sense of respect for the actual business of writing. Feeling discouraged, she wrote to all the editors who had outstanding stories, requesting that they send them back to her. All of the pieces were returned but one. Instead of finding "The Mystery of the Old Stone Well" in her mailbox, she found a check for $60 (*How I Came*, 30), and that was the incentive she needed to continue submitting her works for publication.

In the meantime, in 1951, at age 18, Naylor married and began attending Joliet Junior College, from which she graduated in 1953. From 1953 to 1956 she worked as a clinical secretary at Billings Hospital in Chicago, where the couple lived so that Naylor's husband could pursue a graduate degree in mathematics; her husband, a brilliant scholar, opened new worlds of knowledge to her. In addition to taking classes himself, he fed her a diet of classic literature, including *Vanity Fair*, *War and Peace*, and everything from Dickens and Shakespeare to Balzac and Butler. He introduced her to Freud and to the historian Santayana. Naylor would steep herself in novels of a particular type; for months she would read only nineteenth-century Russian novelists, like Dostoevsky and Tolstoy. Then she would switch to more modern writers, gobbling up books by Sinclair Lewis, Upton Sinclair, and John Steinbeck. Naylor loved this journey into the world of great books; they exposed her to issues that had only been touched upon in her limited childhood reading experiences. She recalls that because these books were not assigned reading for school, she could fling herself into them, reading the last chapter first, not worrying about outlining or answering someone else's questions (*How I Came*, 34–35).

Currently, Naylor spends much time traveling, and writing time is therefore precious. Because of her busy schedule, Naylor continues her exploration of literature through the use of books on tape, listening to everything from *Moll Flanders* and *Jude the Obscure* to *In Cold Blood* and *Rabbit, Run*. When asked during an interview if she considers herself an avid reader, she said,

> No. I love to read, but if I have an extra hour I think, "What should I do with my precious hour?" I am a person who values time; I worship time! Money does not mean that much to me; time does. So, unless I have a headache or am really exhausted, writing always wins out. I think, "Do I really want to read, or wouldn't I rather write?" I *always* write. . . . So I finally have gotten books on tape. I listened to *Snows of Kilimanjaro* coming out here, driving and listening to how "death comes like a hyena" and sits on his chest; books on tape have been my salvation.

Naylor's love of books is a trait she frequently bestows on her characters, who read everything from Plato and Chief Crowfoot to young adult novels such as *Sounder* and *The Outsiders*. She often finds just the right quote from another writer to serve as an introduction, to set the stage, for the story she is about to unfold. *Footprints at the Window* (1981; hereafter cited as *Footprints*), a book about time travel in York, England, during the time of the Black Plague, opens with this citation from Petrarch (1304–1374):

> When has any such thing ever been heard or seen? In what histories has it been read that houses were left vacant, cities

deserted, the country neglected, and a fearful, universal solitude over the whole earth? (*Footprints*, preface)

With those lines readers recognize that they will be thrust into an era in which fear runs rampant and individuals must fend for themselves, a time in which no one can be certain of the future—or even the present. And that sense of uncertainty is exactly what Dan, the 16-year-old protagonist of the "York Trilogy" books, faces as he ventures back in time and struggles with the possibility of inheriting the gene that causes the incurable Huntington's disease.

Naylor also mentions the titles of good books for young adults by other authors within the context of her own stories. She says she does so in order to publicize certain books and authors she feels young people should read. The effect of reading about a favorite character who is, in turn, reading a good book is to promote investigation of those titles by the reader. At the end of *Alice In-Between* (1994; hereafter cited as *A in B*), Naylor lists the books on Alice's summer reading list: *Sydney, Herself* by Colby Rodowsky, *Izzy, Willy-Nilly* by Cynthia Voigt, *After the Rain* by Norma Fox Mazer, *Like Seabirds Flying Home* by Marguerite Murray, *Jacob Have I Loved* by Katherine Paterson, and *Send No Blessings*, a Naylor title. Alice reflects on the importance of reading for young adults facing the world with uncertainty:

> Most of the girls in the books were older than I am, and it was like reading the diaries of older sisters, knowing that if they could get through the problems in *their* lives, I could get through mine. (*A in B*, 141)

Personal Experience as Grist for the Writer's Mill

Naylor's family moved from town to town, causing her to experience some of the kind of uncertainty Dan and Alice face. Naylor lived in eight different neighborhoods in three different states before she started high school. However, there was a stability in her life provided not only through her immediate family life but also by yearly summer visits to both her paternal and maternal grandparents. Her mother's parents lived on a farm in rural Iowa. By temperament they were staid and reserved; they seldom gave hugs or expressed affection in physical ways. Living in isolation from their neighbors, they focused on the business of surviving day by day. Naylor drew on her experiences at their farm to write *To Make a Wee Moon* (1969), one of her earliest novels, and later, *Beetles, Lightly Toasted* (1987).

Naylor's father's parents also lived on a farm—in Marbury, Maryland—but they were outgoing and involved in their community. Her grandfather served as a minister, and her grandmother as a midwife. "Mammaw" gathered some of the local children of Charles County into the car on Sundays to take them to Sunday school. If someone did not have appropriate clothes to wear, Naylor's grandmother would open the trunk and pull out something in the right size from a box of donated clothes, and off they would go to the next house to pick up the next child. This same grandmother took Naylor and her siblings fishing, Naylor recalls fondly, something she finds difficult to imagine her straight-laced German-Scottish grandmother doing.[3]

In *How I Came to Be A Writer* Naylor recalls,

> I never once thought of Maryland as my home, any more than I thought of all the other places I had lived as home, but, quite without knowing it, I was soaking up the setting for future books. . . . By the time I placed a second novel . . . in Marbury, and then a third, . . . I realized this small southern Maryland town had worked its way into my blood. (*How I Came*, 114)

Revelations (1979) and *Unexpected Pleasures* (1986) derive from Naylor's summertime experiences in Marbury. Her southern father, born in Yazoo City, Mississippi, became the role model for the fathers in *Night Cry* (1984), and his father was the patriarch in *A String of Chances* (1982).

Even though Naylor's grandparents had four very unique personalities, her first stories relied on stereotyped characters who acted in predictable ways. Reflecting on these characters, she now says that the grandparents were always "kindly people who sat about with shawls over their shoulders," the mothers "soft-spoken and understanding," the fathers "fair," and the children got into trouble and were sorry when the incident was over (*How I Came*, 33). Naylor credits her education through reading for helping her see the possibilities in writing about what is *not* expected. Exploring this concept, she began to violate stereotypical characterizations and plots. For example, in discussing one of her early efforts, "For Those Who Think Young," Naylor describes how she presents a grandfather who longs to eat pizza and listen to new kinds of music on the radio, but whose children and grandchildren expect him to sit at home by the fire. He has to find ways to trick them into taking him out on the town, to introducing him to new styles of clothes and untried culinary delights; in the process, they become younger in their own mindsets as well (*How I Came*, 36–42).

A poet Naylor knew, who happened to be a neighbor, gave her the classic advice, "Write about what you know." Naylor reflected on the fact that her participation in a youth fellowship group had been a major part of her teenage years, and she decided she could write about adolescents involved in such an organization. But she also realized that, for the most part, church publications were focused on characters who were not very true to life; they often were too good to be real. Naylor remembered her negative reaction to such stories as a teenager and decided to try a humorous approach. She created P. R. Tedesco, a 15-year-old boy—she chose to focus on a male so that her work would appeal to both young men and young women—who narrates the column "First Person Singular," in which he describes his relationships with his parents, the other members of his youth fellowship, his teachers, the minister, the church maintenance man, his girlfriend, and his sister. For close to 25 years Naylor's Tedesco was a staple of Sunday school publications such as *Teen Talk* or *Alive!* (*How I Came*, 55). He reflected on serious themes such as fear, God, and segregation, as well as on the antics of the youth group as it played tricks on the counselor or had to deal with gallons and gallons of soggy ice cream when the social they planned was rained out. Several of Naylor's earliest collections of stories grew out of the Tedesco column, including *Grasshoppers in the Soup* (1965), *Knee Deep in Ice Cream* (1967), and *The Private I* (1969).

Naylor began writing seriously, exploring the Sunday school market and committing herself to supplying the Tedesco column, when she was in her mid-twenties. Between the time of her marriage at 18 and her 23rd birthday, she focused her energies on her marriage and on filling in the gaps in her education based on her husband's suggestions. In addition to her reading program, he introduced her to great music, took her to ethnic restaurants in Chicago, and surrounded her with intellectuals and poets. But, abruptly, when Naylor was only 23, he began to show signs of severe mental illness. One morning he announced that his professors at the university were trying to kill him. From that moment through the next three years, Naylor's life revolved around moving her husband from state to state, trying to find a doctor who could treat him or a hospital in which he could get well. This young woman who could not drive a car, who had never written a check, and who knew nothing of the family's budget nor of tax forms, had to learn survival skills quickly. She had to find means to support herself and her husband while he was incapacitated and unable to work.

As a clinical secretary in a hospital, Naylor tried to learn as much as she could about her husband's illness, eventually diagnosed as paranoid schizophrenia. In 1956 she tried teaching briefly, in Hazelcrest, Illinois, but had to give up that position when her husband, in panic, decided to flee to Minneapolis. She finally borrowed money to move him to a treatment facility on the east coast. From 1958 to 1959 she served as the assistant executive secretary for the Montgomery County Education Association in Maryland. She moved from that position to become an editorial assistant for the *NEA Journal* in Washington, D.C., from 1959 to 1960. While working at all these jobs, she continued to write, sending off story after story tailor-made for various presses, in the hope that she could earn enough to keep afloat financially. For example, her brief experience with elementary school children induced her to write a column for the *NEA Journal* called

"The Light Touch," on the humorous aspects of teaching, such as dealing with all the clothes children bundle into during cold winter months. She would steal an afternoon every so often to sit in an empty church, away from the rush of the world around her and her increasingly difficult husband and his demands. During these interludes she would brainstorm every possible story and article idea she could imagine and every possible publication to which she could send her material, frequently returning to church publications as outlets for her work.

Although Naylor no longer chooses to write for the various church-related publishing houses that first provided an outlet for her material, she speaks of that time in her development as a writer as a time of discovery:

> I discovered I could do this, that I could actually support us in a minimal fashion, and it was the first time that I started thinking, "You know, maybe I could make a living at this writing."

She speaks with fondness of the editors at the Christian presses to whom she sent her prolific outpouring of stories and articles:

> It was a good place to begin because the editors were very helpful, and one of the things that I discovered is that most of the editors are far more liberal than the congregations they represent. They would often send back stories and say, "Oh, I wish I could publish this, but I would be eaten alive if I did." But, I got a lot of feedback from those editors that you don't get when you're sending to the big publishing houses.

Today, Naylor continues to explore themes related to organized religion, faith, and morality in both her humorous and serious works for young adults, a legacy of having spent her youth in a very religious household. She recalls a time when someone gave her older sister a chocolate Easter bunny. Norma sat the candy on her dresser as decoration. Naylor was very envious and says it drove her crazy to see that bunny sitting there, uneaten, every time she passed it by. One day she came home from school, sat on the top step, and ate the entire thing; in revenge, her sister took a pair of scissors and whacked off a huge hunk of Naylor's hair. Marty, in *Shiloh* (1991), also eats his sister Dara Lynn's candy when she receives an Easter bunny and he does not. His mother's response echoes that of Naylor's mother as she tells him Jesus knows who ate the candy and that he will feel better only if he confesses both to Jesus and to his sister.

Naylor's own mother frequently told her children that the only unforgivable act is turning one's back on God, but Naylor grew up to question some of her parents' and their church's teachings about the relationship between God and the individual. Some of this tension is explored later in *Shiloh* when Marty, having made peace with Jesus over the bunny episode, has to decide what God would really have him do when confronted with the knowledge that a neighbor severely mistreats his dog. Naylor finds that she can explore issues that arise when young people question their parents' faith more explicitly in books published by commercial presses than she could with Christian presses. *A String of Chances* is a good example of how Naylor deals with this theme.

When writing for Fortress, Abingdon, and Friendship, however, Naylor discovered the "What if?" formula that she still uses as a way to prompt the flow of ideas:

> I thought church magazines must absolutely publish the worst stuff I've seen in my life. At the time I started writing for them in almost every story the young person got into trouble and saw the error of his ways, and it was so thoroughly boring and awful. I started thinking, "What if the story was written about the parents' problems? What if there was adultery? What if there was mental illness? What if there's overpossessiveness? . . . Those are problems for the child, too." That "What if" question became the basis of most of what I wrote, and these pieces were very different from what the editors were getting. They started publishing them. . . . And that's the point at which I really said, "I *can* make a living this way. I can get ideas fast, and I can think up titles, and I can keep us going."

Today, she still finds the "What if?" question a provocative one that leads her into new plots. *Being Danny's Dog*, 1995, is based in part on the "What ifs" of the situation of Danny, 12, and T. R.,

10. The boys have recently moved to a new development with their mother, who is attempting to start a new life after their father has abandoned the family. Naylor wondered, "What if T.R. feels it is his responsibility to ensure that Danny will not fall in with any 'bad apples,' as their aunt would say?" This musing prompted a story about the struggle of these two boys to help each other into manhood without their father's presence. The idea for another young adult novel, *Ice* (1995), was conceived after Naylor heard an acquaintance describing the horrific sounds associated with an ice storm. Naylor immediately began to wonder, "What if someone were sleeping and heard that noise?"

In the fifties, while earning enough money to pay the rent, buy food, and help with her husband's skyrocketing medical bills, Naylor was learning her craft on the job. One editor returned her submission with the comment, "I want a *story*, not an incident or a simple piece of well done narrative" (*How I Came*, 32). The same editor later advised her that a main character had to have a problem; then, the character had to struggle with that problem and solve it. This editor was adamant that the writer could *not* rely on the sudden appearance of a rich uncle nor on an act of God, a coincidence, nor on an anonymous letter to extricate the character from a difficult situation. Such devices may help the writer create a narrative thread, the editor counseled, but they do not provide the satisfaction of a well-crafted plot with a genuine climax and resolution. Over the years, unity of plot development is the aspect of her craft that Naylor says she has most improved.

When Naylor would begin to run out of ideas, she would reflect on those elements of her own life that meant a great deal to her and try to generate a story from them. Music, for instance, is something she continues to value as a pastime; until recently, one of her hobbies was singing with a local madrigal group. As is true of many other activities she loves, she has now given up ensemble singing to allocate more time to writing. Years ago, however, she drew upon that interest to write a humorous piece about how it feels to be confronted, as a young adult, in church with an unfamiliar hymn. Even her marriage served as the foundation of a book; Naylor eventually felt distant enough from the exhausting experiences of trying to help her husband—and then of making the very difficult decision to divorce him—to write *Crazy Love: An Autobiographical Account of Marriage and Madness* (1977). Later on, wondering how a young person would cope with a parent who becomes incapacitated through mental illness led her to write *The Keeper* (1986), a young adult novel in which Nick's father displays all the symptoms Naylor's first husband exhibited.

In 1960, Naylor married for the second time. This new husband was as patient and supportive as her first spouse was compulsive and demanding. She and Rex Naylor, a speech pathologist, have two children. Jeff was born in 1962, and Michael in 1966. The ups and downs of family life spawned many writing ideas and became the basis for an amusing column in an adult church magazine. These columns, collected later in the volume *In Small Doses* (1979), feature a family of five—a husband, Ralph; two sons, Jack and Peter; a daughter, Susan; and a mother as narrator—solidly grounded in Naylor's own family. The names were changed to prevent her sons from feeling embarrassed by seeing their family's escapades in print, and the daughter was a creative addition designed to round out the family composition. Most of the pieces deal with various aspects of parenting, offering, in a wry tone, reminders that parents often do best to show their children that they believe in them and value them as individuals. For example, in "S.Y.K. Day," the mother reflects that Jack's behavior proves what she has always believed: "Kids want to know you care about them. Give them a mile, sometimes, and they'll settle for an inch" (*In Small Doses*, 57). Later, in "Of Time and Christmas Past," two days after Christmas, Pete is bored. His mother keeps reminding him of his new toys, making suggestions about ways he can occupy his time. Finally he says he just wants "something we can do together" (*In Small Doses*, 61). Two hours later, when they are both up to their elbows in flour, and cinnamon buns are baking in the oven, she reminds herself that sharing time is more important than the rush of Christmas activity.

Naylor recalls being embarrassed during a TV interview in which the host went on and on about how *real* the characters from *In Small Doses* felt to him, remarking especially upon Susan's authenticity. Naylor finally confessed that she had made up Susan, that she did not have a daughter. The host refused to believe her and insisted that the book was proof of the daughter's existence. As Naylor notes, "Ah. The power of the printed word!"[4]

Naylor often remarks how much fun it is that her own family members are so different from each other because they each bring a unique perspective and varied interests to family get-togethers. Jeff and Mike are as different as Jack and Pete. One is somewhat quiet and more introspective; the other is extroverted. One attended a small liberal arts college; the other chose a large state university. One became a Quaker; the other describes himself as an agnostic. "They each have an original sense of humor, and yet," she writes, "we all enjoy each other, and the differences between us just add to our breadth of experience—give us each a chance to enjoy some aspect of life we know little about."[5] She continues to draw upon her own family experiences as grist for her writing. *The Grand Escape* (1993) features Naylor's cats Marco and Ulysses as role models for feline heroes Marco and Polo. After Ulysses underwent surgery for a massive stomach tumor (which turned out to be a ball composed of 40 feet of Christmas ribbon, 11 rubber bands, hair, and grass), he was banned from the outside world but still longed to escape. The novel relates the adventures of Marco and Polo, who manage to elude their masters and then must fend for themselves in the great outdoors of suburbia, confronting their own worst fear—riding in a car—in the process.

An ability to delight in the little dramas of daily life is evident throughout Naylor's work. At one point, the mother from *In Small Doses* longs for someone to start a company that will do errands such as pet-sitting (for Marco and Ulysses), picking up clothes at the cleaners, getting the lawn mower sharpened, or buying a new washer for the kitchen faucet. Reconsidering, she recognizes that she might not really want to give up the privilege of helping her daughter pull off a snowy boot or of shopping for ripe avocados.

> Perhaps it is the minutia of life that makes us appreciate the rest of living. If we'd never experienced the chore of scrubbing a roasting pan, could dinner at a restaurant ever taste so exquisite? And what could match the satisfaction of balancing a bank statement with twenty-seven checks outstanding and have it come out right the first time? (*In Small Doses*, 160)

Learning to find joy in small accomplishments and in the minutia of living is something Naylor practiced during the difficult years with her first husband as he struggled with mental illness. This skill plus the recognition of the value of humor in coping with endless details are strengths evident even in her early work. Naylor has honed these abilities over the years. She has written for magazines with titles such as *Woodmen of the World*, *The New York Mirror*, *Teaching Tools*, and *Elementary English*. She has composed funny stories and serious ones, plays, advice columns, and poems. Her audiences have been kindergarten children and retired senior citizens. And her subjects have been far-reaching: One story might be about a teenager who discovers she has diabetes and begins to wallow in self-pity until her friends help her see that the disease is just one part of who she is; another story might be about a girl who has been asked out by two boys for the same event. Naylor wrote to support herself while she attended American University, from which she graduated in 1963 with a degree in psychology.

The Writer Tackles "The Book"— and Becomes a Novelist

After several years of full-time writing, Naylor finally decided in 1964 to tackle the one thing that she had been terrified of: a book. Why was she apprehensive? She wondered if she would get bored working on a long-term project. She worried that the book might not sell after she had invested a great deal of time and energy into it. She was concerned that she might begin writing about characters whom she would eventually come to dislike. But her older sister had written to her, asking why she had never produced a book. Naylor says,

> Since I had always envied my older sister, it sort of rankled that she wasn't giving enough credit to just writing short stories. So, to prove I could, I collected nine short stories and put them together [as a book], and I sent them to Abingdon Press, the Methodist publishing house, because the Methodists have missionaries, and though the stories are not specifically religious, they each take place in a foreign country. And I was right. They took it [*The Galloping Goat and Other Stories*, 1965] and I was *still* scared. So, for my second book, I simply took a collection of teenage stories I had written. *Grasshoppers in the Soup* (1965) also came out in 1965. It wasn't until *What the Gulls Were Singing* (1967) [that I tried a novel]. It is very episodic. I simply sat down and made a list of all the things that could happen at the ocean, and I then divided them into chapters.

What the Gulls Were Singing is a family story based on Naylor's recollections of her own family vacations at the beach. She admits she tried to throw in *everything*, every possible plot twist, from encounters with a gypsy to the damage and danger of a hurricane. She sent it to an editor at Follett who rejected it. Sensing possibilities in the manuscript, however, the editor told her to find a central theme and to rewrite from just one character's point of view instead of using third-person omniscient. Seven months later, the editor at Follett bought the manuscript, and Naylor the novelist was born.

Although she continued to publish short-story collections through the mid-1980s (*A Triangle Has Four Sides* [1984] was the last of these), after the sale of *What the Gulls Were Singing* Naylor began focusing on the writing of novels, both for children and for young adults, and children's picture books. She describes how, when her younger son was two or three, she engaged a babysitter one day a week. She would go to the library, write for eight hours, and come home with a stack of picture books to read with Michael. For years, he thought those books were the product of her time away from him, and he was devastated to learn they were not![6]

Naylor continued to maintain her ties with the various Christian presses that had been so good to her up to this point in her career. *When Rivers Meet* (1968), for example, was an assignment given to her by a committee of 10 individuals at Friendship Press, each of whom had a different idea about what should be included in the book. It is a tale of a young man of Ethiopia's royal family who comes to a Midwestern town to live as an exchange student for a year. He finds himself embroiled in the town's growing racial tensions. Because his visit was sponsored by a church group, his presence and its catalytic effect prompt the church members, youth and adults alike, to consider the role of the church in changing the status quo. Naylor says of this book, "Oh, that is the worst book!" She notes, in hindsight,

> I never should have taken it on. It's the one book I'm just really embarrassed about. I didn't even remember there was an Ethiopian in it. I've just blocked it out of my mind. . . . I've never been to Ethiopia; I'm not sure I've ever met an Ethiopian. Why would I ever choose to write about something I know so little about? But, I was still new, and I was still writing church stories, and when you write a short story you can take on something like that because it's very short and you can just stick to a few points you know, and you don't have to go into it in depth. But to write a whole book about an Ethiopian . . . ! I just would never, ever tackle something like that now.

This experience notwithstanding, Naylor felt more positive about *Making It Happen* (1970), whose main character is based on P. R. Tedesco from her church paper column, "First Person Singular." Having given Tedesco voice once a week for many years, Naylor felt she knew this young man intimately. She says the novel "almost wrote itself" (*How I Came*, 62).

Open to suggestions from the various editors with whom she worked, Naylor was often encouraged to try genres and new markets. For example, when a new publisher, J. Phillip O'Hara, wrote to her, asking if she would author a nonfiction book on the Amish, Naylor admits that she did not really want to undertake the project, noting that she is not especially interested in writing nonfiction.

But it was a new company, and I hadn't had that many books out, and I thought, "This is a chance to try something different, and in the end I really enjoyed doing it. Just the inconsistencies in the lives of the Amish, the contradictions, were extremely interesting, and I thought it was well done in the end. A lot of people think it's a novel."

In 1974 Naylor's evolving skill as a fiction writer produced *An Amish Family,* in which the lives of a fictional Amish family unfold in narrative fashion. While telling their story, Naylor weaves in detail after detail about Amish courtship and wedding rituals, funeral customs, barn raisings, schooling, and religious beliefs and practices.

Naylor uses the same storytelling technique in the various advice books she wrote for Abingdon Press on topics such as *Getting Along in Your Family* (1976), *Getting Along with Your Friends* (1979), *Getting Along with Your Teachers* (1981), and *How to Find Your Wonderful Someone* (Fortress, 1972). In these early books, readers are drawn into vignettes about a child in conflict with a sibling, or about a teenager upset over dating issues, and then Naylor delivers words of wisdom on how the protagonist might deal with the situation.

Although Naylor continued to send short-story collections and even a few novels to Christian presses, by the mid-seventies most of her work was being published by commercial presses. After *What the Gulls Were Singing,* she published several other novels and picture books with Follett, and Silver Burdett picked up several of her children's books. In 1975 *Witch's Sister* came out with Atheneum, and Naylor has been publishing consistently— although not exclusively—with that company ever since. She has contracts with Atheneum for works in progress to be printed through the late nineties.

Naylor is known for her ability to write for a variety of audiences in a variety of styles. Not only her sensitive portrayal of teenagers wrestling with difficult issues but also her ear for dialogue, her sense of humor, and her consistent awareness of the loneliness of adolescence have won her a place in the ranks of the best-loved, most highly regarded contemporary writers. The rest of this text will explore in more depth Naylor's talents as a humorist, as an author able to grapple with serious themes, and as an individual committed to putting words on paper and serving her reading public—particularly the young adult.

2. On Surviving the Middle Years— or Naylor In-Between and the "Alice" Books

Alice McKinley was ushered into the public eye in 1985 when Naylor published *The Agony of Alice* with Atheneum. Marketed as a children's novel, it was named an American Library Association Notable Children's Book. *Alice* immediately acquired a faithful, loving readership of upper elementary and middle school girls, and Naylor found herself unexpectedly deciding to continue the story of this young girl's journey into womanhood.

In many ways the "Alice" books represent Naylor at her best. These titles show her gift for writing about and for younger adolescents who feel caught in the middle in so many ways—in the middle of childhood longings and adult responsibilities, in the middle of physical changes, and in the middle of tensions caused both by the desire to be independent and by the need to belong to a group. Although Naylor has written for younger children and adults with critical success, it is in the Alice books that her skill in characterization, her ear for dialogue, and her sensitivity to adolescent concerns come together in tightly focused, well-developed tales about a strong, feisty young woman who in many ways is the prototype of other Naylor protagonists.

Introducing Alice McKinley

Who is Alice McKinley? She is the only female in a small family consisting of an older brother, Lester (eight years her senior), and a father, Ben, who manages The Melody Inn, a music store in Silver Spring, Maryland. Alice tells us, in *The Agony of Alice* (1985; hereafter cited as *A of A*), that her parents lived in Tennessee originally but moved to Chicago before she was born. Her mother's death, when Alice was four, prompted her father to consider another move. At age six, Alice found herself in Takoma Park, Maryland; when she turned eleven and was ready to begin sixth grade, her father moved the family to Silver Spring. Alice's father plays the violin and the flute; Lester plays an electric guitar. Tone deaf, Alice is mortified by her inability to match a pitch and carry a tune. Her friend Patrick—a drummer—helps her discover, however, that she has a strong sense of rhythm.

Alice's Aunt Sally, who lives in Chicago with Uncle Milt, took care of Alice after her mother died. She is the person to whom Alice turns for answers to questions she assumes other girls ask their mothers. However, dear Aunt Sally is always at least 10 years behind the times, so Alice is often puzzled by her aunt's well-intentioned advice. Aunt Sally's unbounded enthusiasm over her niece's physical development also baffles Alice, whose own observations on the changes in her body are understated. For example, while staying with Aunt Sally, Alice's menstrual period begins. Aunt Sally gushes, "Your very first time! My, such an occasion—the beginning of all the privileges and responsibilities of womanhood!" Alice thinks, "That was really weird, and I didn't know what to say. I didn't want any privileges of womanhood. I just wanted some sanitary napkins" (*A of A*, 113). If Alice is lucky, Aunt Sally's grown daughter Carol will intervene and offer useful advice in place of Aunt Sally's old-fashioned perspectives.

Aunt Sally and cousin Carol notwithstanding, motherless Alice worries: "I never quite know exactly who I'm supposed to be like or how I'm supposed to act. What I need, I guess, is a pattern, a road map; but all I've got is a father and Lester, and Lester has been no help to me whatsoever" (*A of A*, 11). When she was seven, for example, she overheard older girls talking about periods during recess. She asked her brother to explain periods and was told that they were commas "without tails." Even then Alice knew something was fishy about Lester's answer; girls of her acquaintance would not spend their entire recess discussing punctuation!

After moving to Silver Spring, Alice becomes best friends with Elizabeth Price, who lives across the street, and Pamela Jones. Eventually these two girls compose a sort of support group along with Lester's girlfriends, Marilyn and Crystal, and Aunt Sally and Carol. They all help Alice cope with the changes that come with puberty: buying a first bra, wearing deodorant, getting pierced ears, kissing a boy for the first time, and determining how to be true to one's own values while maintaining status with the "in crowd." Marilyn even teaches her about caring for her cuticles; up until then, Alice confesses, she did not even know she *had* cuticles (*A of A*, 71).

The search for an appropriate adult female role model and the importance of the mother-daughter relationship are two themes Naylor explores in all of the Alice books and other young adult novels. These were themes of significance to Naylor throughout her own adolescence. Her mother, Lura, a farm girl from a very large family in rural Iowa, had to leave home and board with a German family in town in order to attend high school. Because of the language barrier in that house, Naylor's mother felt lonely and isolated. Through her inner strength and determination, Lura managed to complete high school, attend a religious college, and become a teacher, maintaining some of her country mannerisms all the while. Even though Naylor loved her mother and felt loved in return, she was embarrassed by Lura's rustic ways as she grew into young adulthood. Perceiving a narrowness of experience on her mother's part, young Naylor wanted to look different and be different and pursue broader horizons, so she searched for alternatives to her mother's lifestyle. Given this background, Naylor skillfully conveys just how important it is to Alice to have someone guide her through the bewildering array of options and the overwhelming number of decisions she faces as a young woman growing up in a family of men.

Agonizing with Alice

In *The Agony of Alice*, Alice, to her dismay, finds herself assigned to the homely, large, and oddly shaped Mrs. Plotkin for sixth grade. Mrs. Plotkin takes Alice under her wing, accepts her, and seems to understand her awkwardness. To help her find a niche in the new school, she asks Alice to be the classroom's alternate "safety," or student crossing guard, which means Alice has a reason for being close to Miss Cole, head of the safety patrol and whom Alice adores for her glittering beauty. Mrs. Plotkin also asks her students to keep a journal of their important thoughts and feelings. Alice names hers "The Agonies of Alice," and in it she records the many embarrassing things that happen to her throughout that tumultuous sixth-grade year. Eventually, Alice realizes that although she is surrounded by a host of possible female role models, it is actually Mrs. Plotkin whom she wants to emulate. Mrs. Plotkin's kind heart, her wit, and her expertise as a teacher win Alice over in the end.

During this same period, Alice and Lester's relationship begins to mature. She reaches out to comfort him after Marilyn breaks up with him, and is amazed that they are able to have a complete conversation without being rude or teasing each other—a precursor of one of the themes Naylor continues to explore in the later Alice books.

In a *School Library Journal* starred review of this first Alice book, Caroline Ward praises Naylor: "The lively style exhibits a deft touch at capturing the essence of an endearing heroine growing up without a mother."[1] *Booklist* also gave *The Agony of Alice* a highlighted review:

> Although the resolution is a little too easy, Naylor's characters are drawn with subtlety and affection, and there is no heavy moralizing. . . . A wonderfully funny and tender story that will make readers smile with wry recognition.[2]

The Reading Teacher selected the book for its "Children's Choices for 1986" listing, praising "its realistic and humorous style" and its "important statement about the importance of role models."[3]

Naylor's "deft touch" is evident most readily in the excerpts from Alice's journal, in her interior monologues as she narrates and reflects upon her experiences, and in her conversations with those who compose her world. For instance, when Alice's dad asks her what kind of new clothes she wants to start sixth grade, Alice says she wants to buy real Levi jeans in a store; in the past, she has ordered out of the Sears catalog. Delegated to lead the shopping expedition, Lester attempts to fit her in the boys' department. When all the jeans he selects are way too long and much too large in the waist, he tells Alice, "Maybe you've got a strange body or something" (*A of A*, 22), which causes Alice to burst into tears. A female clerk comes to Alice's rescue, guides her to the girls' department, and makes her feel okay about herself again.

That good feeling evaporates suddenly, however, when Alice opens the door to the wrong dressing room. She is confronted by a red-headed boy wearing blue underwear who stares at her, mouth open. Unbeknownst to Alice, this is her first meeting with Patrick, another staple of the Alice books. Unaware of how significant Patrick's presence will be in her life, Alice bolts out of sight into the right dressing room and decides she will never come out. Once Lester gets her home, Alice has a "long, hard think" about herself and begins to worry that instead of growing up, she is growing ever more babyish. She uses a chart to try to determine whether this is so. In one column she lists all the things she has learned to do that seem to indicate some progress toward maturity; in the other column, she notes those actions that signal regression:

Forward	Backward
Make Kraft dinner	Ate crayons
Empty lint trap on dryer	Wrote poem to milkman
Remove splinters	Donald Sheavers
Eat squash	Rude to Elizabeth Price
Raise guppies	Can't buy bra
	Opened wrong door at Gap (*A of A*, 24)

Unfortunately, Alice looks at her chart and is dismayed to realize the "backward" column is winning.

As Alice marches through her sixth-grade year, she updates the chart, noting when she learns to chew gum with her mouth closed—a forward marker—and how she wiped her fingers with what turned out to be moo-shu pork pancakes at a Chinese restaurant—definitely a backward marker. The specifics here—the details of learning to eat squash compared to not being able to buy a bra—show Naylor's recognition of how concrete younger adolescents are in their thinking and of how the smallest aspect of daily life becomes the source of endless contemplation as the child struggles to figure out how to do things right.

Naylor is also adept at capturing the acuteness of the embarrassment sixth graders feel when they try to do something grown-up but overdo it. In an interview with Tim Poddell, Naylor says what she remembers most about her adolescence is being fearful. Whereas other writers claim they can recall what was happening in their lives by rereading books of importance to them at various stages of development, Naylor notes that she recollects different ages by remembering things that worried her at different times.[4]

Alice, like Naylor, is a worrier. For example, Alice almost never gets mail addressed directly to her; thus, she claims as her own all mail sent to "occupant." On a Wednesday afternoon, she opens a sampler of "Maharaja's Magic, the only perfume you will ever need." Alice sticks the card in with her tee shirts so they will smell good. Unfortunately, the response to her experiment is not what she had hoped. Elizabeth Price tells her the smell is terribly strong. Alice considers going home to shower, change, and hang all her tee shirts out to air, but she walks into the classroom anyway. Immediately, Pamela Jones, whom Alice has considered a friend, reacts to her presence.

> "What stinks?" said Pamela.
> I didn't even have time to answer before somebody else said, "Euuyuk!"

The boys get wind of Alice's interesting odor and start pretending to be sick, causing the girls to giggle. Alice considers this probably the worst day of her life. She knows she cannot go home at noon even to change, because doing so would be an admission of embarrassment. So, she recalls, "I played soccer instead, in hopes that all that running around would air the tee shirt out. What it did was mix some sweat with Maharaja's Magic so that, when I came in after lunch, I smelled like the Maharaja's horse. I wanted to disappear" (*A of A*, 55–56).

Wearing perfume to school becomes yet another item in the "backward" column of Alice's chart. Naylor knows exactly how direct, and therefore cruel, sixth graders can be in such situations, and describes perfectly how Alice feels about herself.

It is Mrs. Plotkin who continues to accept Alice as herself, with all her faults; she does not ask about the perfume, she merely opens a window. Then she asks Alice if she would like to help out in the classroom after school, providing her a sense of belonging even when she is feeling the most excluded. With her dramatic voice, Mrs. Plotkin lures Alice into the world of stories—echoes of Naylor's own parents' gifts. Through her expression alone, the teacher is able to reveal to her listeners exactly what is going on in a character's mind and heart. It takes Alice a while, though, to admit she enjoys story time. During the whole first week of school, she pretends to do her homework instead of listening. But when Mrs. Plotkin just carries on, not saying anything to Alice to embarrass her, Alice realizes how in tune Mrs. Plotkin is with her feelings about being new. Eventually she carves *"Life is unfair"* (*A of A*, 77) on her desktop; she comes to think it is a shame that Mrs. Plotkin's homely looks disguise her wonderfully kind heart.

It is also Mrs. Plotkin who helps Alice begin to understand her strengths. In Alice's journal, in the margin of the page on which Alice has described her conversation with Lester after his breakup with Marilyn, Mrs. Plotkin tells Alice that she writes well and thanks her for sharing her gift for words (*A of A*, 77). For the first time, Alice feels both embarrassed and happy simultaneously, and readers realize she has gained an important insight into what being grown up means. She begins to understand Mrs. Plotkin's statement that it is fine to have secrets, as long as one is not hiding anything from oneself (*A of A*, 126).

Again, it is Mrs. Plotkin who takes Alice in hand when Alice ruins the Christmas play. In the lead role is Pamela, who possesses the singing skill that Alice lacks. In her own role as a bramble bush, jealous Alice yanks on Pamela's hair in the middle of the performance. Mrs. Plotkin neither scolds nor asks that typical adult question, "*Why* did you do that, Alice?" Instead, she comments, "I don't think you feel very good about what happened, Alice." She further points out that it seems Alice "is angry at Pamela for wanting the very things that you want. It's not so horrible to want to be special" (*A of A*, 85). Alice confesses her fear that she is regressing. Mrs. Plotkin replies simply that everyone has to grow older, but that process is more difficult for some than for others.

The new year arrives, and Alice concludes that Mrs. Plotkin is changing. Alice believes the teacher has one of the most beautiful voices she has ever heard, and she is convinced Mrs. Plotkin looks a lot prettier than when they first met. On the last day before summer vacation, Mrs. Plotkin sends her home from school with a wonderful gift—her great-grandmother's ring, still a bit large for Alice's finger, with its cut on the knuckle and dirt under the nail. Alice knows that she will grow into it—both physically and metaphorically. The reader perceives that—in learning that "things aren't always what they seem"—she has already started that growth process. The surface beauty of the glittering Miss Cole, the other sixth-grade teacher whom Alice had hoped to have, cannot compare with the inner loveliness of pear-shaped Mrs. Plotkin. Alice understands that Mrs. Plotkin has not changed. Rather, it is her own, more mature perception of her teacher that is different.

The Agony of Patrick

Part of Alice's agony in sixth grade comes from not quite knowing how to deal with Patrick, the boy Alice and her readers first see wearing underwear and socks during the shopping fiasco. Alice next encounters him on the way home from school one day, when she steps off the curb into the path of an oncoming mail truck. Patrick, the safety assigned to that corner, pulls her out of harm's way and tells her she is not to cross the street until he gives the signal. As they look at each other's faces, Alice realizes that a) he is the boy with the blue underwear, and b) he knows who she is. He quickly turns away. Alice begins running and does not stop until she reaches her house. Their joint embarrassment leads them to develop an unofficial system: Whenever Alice happens to look toward him, Patrick turns away, and if he should look at her, she turns out of his line of sight. Alice figures that if she ever tried to say something to him, something dumb would come out of her mouth, like "How are your Fruit-of-the-Looms this morning?" (*A of A*, 49). It seems better all the way around to avoid contact of any sort.

When Valentine's Day rolls around, Alice takes her box of cards home and, to her surprise, finds an envelope addressed to "Alice M." decorated with hearts and roses and airplanes with red stripes on their wings. Inside is a card with the hand-printed message, "I like you a lot" (*A of A*, 90). For days, Alice tries to figure out who uses a pen with blue ink (eight boys) and who draws airplane wings with red stripes. She begins taking a comb to school so she can untangle her hair; she sorts through her shirts, puts those with missing buttons or holes aside, and wears only the nicer ones to school.

One day Alice is trying to talk with Pamela, who is ignoring her after a fight. As they approach the crossing at Patrick's corner, Alice hears his voice calling out to her, sees a Milky Way flying through the air, and catches it. She does not connect flying Milky Ways with flying planes until the next day, when she sees the mural Miss Cole's class has done on communication. There they are, blue airplanes with red-striped wings. Casually asking a member of the class who had drawn them, she learns that it is Patrick, of the blue underwear, who had sent her a valentine. The next morning Patrick throws her another Milky Way. Alice recalls, "This time I was so nervous I dropped it, and then I saw Patrick smiling and I smiled back; and after that, I guess, we were going together." Patrick joins her, uninvited, for lunch, which causes Elizabeth to stare—boys do not sit with the girls. But Patrick wants to know where Alice lives and whether he can ride his bike over to visit her, and she is impressed with his matter-of-fact, "just like that" approach to this change in their relationship (*A of A*, 94–95).

While Alice is embarrassed just by being alive, Patrick is never embarrassed. He wears the blue underwear to school for Halloween as part of his Superman costume, for instance. Whereas Alice has difficulty finding topics for conversation, Patrick always has something to say. Alice has never been on a plane and has traveled only as far as Tennessee; Patrick, on the contrary, has lived in Germany, Spain, and Japan, and flies every summer to Oregon *by himself* to visit his grandparents. When Alice complains to her father that she has led a boring life, he cooks an exotic meal of squid, since that is something Alice mentions Patrick has eaten, and offers her the chance to take the train *alone* to Chicago to stay with Aunt Sally over spring break. In Chicago, she has her hair cut, buys some new clothes, and gets her period. When she returns home, Patrick comes over, bearing a box of Whitman's chocolate-covered cherries, and their relationship seems about to take a new turn. Patrick had left the box of candy sitting in the sun all afternoon, so the two young people have to eat them with a spoon. Alice says, "I'd scoop up one, then he'd take one, and when we were through, I knew he was going to kiss me" (*A of A*, 129).

Naylor knows exactly how the moment of the first kiss plays out. The players involved seldom move in well-choreographed synchronization; rarely are they truly swept away by passion. The reality is that the first kiss is a time of awkwardness and panic. Alice's hands begin to tingle. Realizing she could easily burst into giggles, she sternly tells herself to just get it over with and thus stops the glider to facilitate the kiss. As it turns out, she need not have worried. Patrick leans over so close to her that she can smell the chocolate on his breath. But then the glider begins to move again, and when she looks at Patrick, he is staring straight ahead. Alice is thus amazed to discover that worldly Patrick cannot quite get up the nerve to actually kiss her (*A of A*, 130).

Alice begins to chatter wildly about everything that crosses her mind, perceiving that she needs to help Patrick realize that his failure did not matter. She also knows that if she runs out of conversation, Patrick will try again: That is the kind of boy he is. Sure enough, he begins to fidget until he gets his arm around Alice's back. They both close their eyes and lean clumsily forward, and their lips "collided." But even though Alice thinks this kiss is probably one of the shortest on record, she knows that she will write "Kissed Patrick" in the forward column of her chart. And, given the relief Patrick demonstrates, she thinks he may have a list somewhere on which he will note "Kissed Alice" as an accomplishment right under "Count in Japanese" (*A of A*, 130).

Naylor knows just how important the first kiss is to a young adolescent, and she captures this momentous event—in all its awkwardness—with a tender realism. Vicariously learning to cope with the unknown through the adventures of Alice and company, young readers thus discover what to expect when their turn comes. Such empathetic writing constitutes a source of comfort for young people at a trying age.

Moving Beyond Sixth Grade

The Agony of Alice provides an introduction to many of the themes and issues Naylor continues to develop throughout the "Alice" series. Alice and her friends will have to accept their constantly maturing bodies. As they wander through the ups and downs, the ins and outs of relationships with other girls and with boys, Naylor explores the themes of friendship, loyalty, and romance. As Alice grows older, so do her father and Lester, allowing Naylor to elaborate on her themes through other perspectives and to explore the meaning of family ties. The issue of choosing the right role model evolves throughout the series; the various Alice books also deal with meaningful secondary themes, such as the nature of bravery or responsibility.

Dealing with Puberty

Having difficulty accepting the fact that she is a physical being, prim Elizabeth never wants to talk about the realities of being a female. In *Alice in April* (1993; hereafter cited as *April*), Elizabeth's mother is expecting—a situation that embarrasses Elizabeth. "Everybody knows they did *that!*" (*April*, 85) she wails, and not until Alice points out that even the *pope* is here because his parents engaged in similar activity does Elizabeth calm down. Pamela, on the other hand, is always three steps ahead of everyone else. In *Alice in Rapture, Sort Of* (1989; hereafter cited as *Rapture*), Elizabeth advises Alice never to answer the phone right after the first ring when anticipating a phone call from a boy, asserting that the girl who does so sounds too eager. Pamela, however, maintains that the girl has to answer before the third ring; otherwise, the boy will think she does not care (*Rapture*, 5). When the subject of French kissing arises, Pamela acts as though she knows all about it, having studied the subject through reading magazines. Elizabeth refuses to listen to the discussion. Alice, on the other hand, has pragmatic concerns. She wonders how many times you have to brush your teeth before you are ready to French-kiss. She decides she will need to start planning early in the morning and then watch what she eats all day so that her mouth will not "taste like onions or anything" (*Rapture*, 7).

Alice is not unusually narcissistic, but, like most adolescents, she is concerned with her image. She periodically analyzes and compares herself to Pamela's sophisticated look and Elizabeth's innocent mien. Most young adults can identify with the ache in her heart as she examines her body, finding fault with her skinny legs, bony knees, and big feet. She reflects that, although she has no hips, she might have at least felt good about starting to develop a bustline "if my lips weren't so thin and my hair wasn't so straight. . . . I'm not really ugly. Just so terribly—*Alice*" (*Rapture*, 6).

The contrast between prim and proper Elizabeth and fast-track Pamela serves throughout the series to put Alice in context. She is the middle-of-the-road member of the group, always struggling to mediate between the two extremes represented by her best friends. For example, in *Alice in Rapture, Sort Of*, all three girls have boyfriends, and they spend their evenings walking through town showing off their status as couples, sometimes stopping at the playground, sometimes getting ice cream. Pamela and Mark wrap their arms around each other's backs and stroll with their hands in each other's pockets. Elizabeth and her boyfriend chastely hold hands. Alice and Patrick walk with their arms around each other's waists.

In *Rapture,* Elizabeth's difficulties in acknowledging the reality of bodily functions emerge in concrete and astonishing ways. She avoids chewing when she is around her boyfriend because she is embarrassed to realize that he will know she is swallowing, processing her food, a "disgusting" process in her opinion: "You put food in your mouth and it gets all mixed up with spit and you chew it up into a revolting mess and swallow it" (*Rapture,* 76). Elizabeth cannot imagine engaging in this act in front of *boys.*

Alice and Pamela cannot bear to think that Elizabeth is giving up eating. Good friends that they are, they say that if she will eat her ice cream, they will distract the boys, which they do by balancing plastic spoons on their noses. The boys join in, and Elizabeth successfully eats her ice cream in public. But readers know she will continue to be perplexed and embarrassed by her own body. When such topics arise in conversation, her standard comment is "Don't even talk about it!"

The theme of dealing with developing bodies is central to *Alice in April.* Once again Alice finds herself in the middle of the continuum between Pamela and Elizabeth. In this book, a group of seventh-grade boys decides to give all the girls nicknames. Each girl is assigned the name of a state, the topography of which reflects her budding breast line. Elizabeth is dubbed "Illinois." Trying to comfort her, Pamela and Alice squeeze onto the couch next to Elizabeth, and Pamela says,

> "It's not really that bad! There are *some* hills in Illinois, really! There just aren't any mountains, that's all."
> Elizabeth sniffled again. "Are you s-s-sure?"
> "She's right!" I said. "I used to live there. There are lots of big hills that . . . well, maybe not *big* hills, but . . . more like slopes. Not ski slopes, of course, but well . . . you know those places where the road goes up and down?"
> Elizabeth's face was clouding up again.

"Listen," said Pamela. "It could be *much* worse! You could have been Louisiana, you know. Now *that's* flat."

"Or Delaware," I said. "Feel sorry for the girl who gets Delaware." (*April*, 8–9)

Seeking to help Elizabeth, Alice tells Lester about the states and asks him what a girl could say to a boy that would embarrass him in the same way. He advises her to say, "Don't worry; some day the other one will drop" (*April*, 11). However, he will not elaborate on the meaning of the phrase. Alice pluckily tackles her father for an explanation. Very matter-of-factly he replies,

"Probably refers to the testicles, Al," he said. "Sometimes boys are born with a testicle up the groin instead of down in the scrotum. In most of these cases it descends soon after birth, but in some boys this doesn't happen till puberty; I'd imagine they're very self conscious about it." (*April*, 11)

Alice is amazed to learn that boys ever have to worry about such personal things; revealing her good heart, she resolves that no matter what a boy might call her, she will never use Lester's phrase in retaliation because it is just too cruel.

Still, Alice is hurt when, shortly after Elizabeth is named, Pamela finds out she has been dubbed "Wyoming"—but she herself still has no state status. Being ignored feels worse than being called "Delaware." Patrick and the males in her family tell her over and over again that the whole naming scheme is silly and does not deserve her attention, yet she becomes obsessed. When Brian Brewster finally says, "Hey, Wyoming! Hey, North Carolina and Illinois!" (*April*, 127), it is clear that "North Carolina" refers to Alice. She panics and races to the library to find out as much as possible about that state's geographical features. Learning that Mt. Mitchell, the highest peak east of the Mississippi, is in North Carolina, Alice wants to scream or dance:

I stood straight, head up, chest out, my Mount Mitchells protruding proudly out in front, and for just a moment that afternoon, when I first stepped out of the shower in the gym, I didn't wrap the towel around me. (*April*, 131)

Later, in *Alice In-Between* (1994; hereafter cited as *A in B*), the girls have developed enough to realize they *have* to wear bras all the time. According to Ann Landers, if a pencil slid under a girl's breast stays in place, the girl should never go without a bra. As soon as the trio discover this test, Pamela, of course, unbuttons her shirt right in front of the others, slides a pencil into place, raises her arms, and announces "Ta da!" because the pencil stays put. Elizabeth cannot bear the thought of having her best friends see her body, so she hides in the bathroom to take the test. When she emerges, she admits, "The only way I could get the pencil to stay up there was with toothpaste" (*A in B*, 26). When it is Alice's turn, Alice decides she cannot follow Elizabeth's lead; if she goes into the bathroom, she is afraid she will turn into her Aunt Sally, who is always conservative and even embarrassed about the physical aspects of being alive. Screwing up her courage, she takes off her tee shirt and then her bra, which is, in fact, "a sports bra, if you want the truth. I don't think Elizabeth had ever seen my breasts close up before, and she turned pink and looked away, but Pamela just tucked the pencil up under my left breast. I was about to say, 'Ta da!' too, but the pencil suddenly fell to the floor" (*A in B*, 36).

After a second attempt with the pencil leads to the same result, Alice is somewhat chagrined to think that she is neither *bra* nor *braless* but somewhere in between. She decides to ask her dad and Lester if there is a male equivalent for the pencil test. It says a good deal for their relationship that she is able to talk so frankly about puberty issues with them, although she derives little comfort from her father's assurance that *all* females at some point are caught between childhood and womanhood. Alice, speaking for so many adolescents, informs him, "Well, it's a crummy place to be" (*A in B*, 38).

In *Alice the Brave* (1995; hereafter cited as *Brave*), all three girls have so filled out that they no longer worry too much about their proportions. Instead, other aspects of puberty demand their attention, particularly boy-girl interactions. After reading out loud to her friends from *Tales from the Arabian Nights*, Elizabeth feels so guilty about the curiosity evoked by the tantalizing descriptions of "Yemeni wrigglings" and "Nubian lasciviousness" that she goes to confession. Assured by her priest that inquisitiveness about bodily functions is okay, Elizabeth learns to kiss and flirt. On the first day of eighth grade, she even goes to school dressed in tight new jeans with the second button of her shirt undone. Pamela, first to have a boyfriend, is first to break up. Alice goes with her father to visit his assistant manager, Janice Sherman, who is hospitalized for a hysterectomy. Alice is present when another store worker announces she is getting married in a few days—and is pregnant. Thus, Alice begins to get a sense for issues of sexuality larger than those she has experienced in her relationship with Patrick. Nevertheless, she assures her father in the last line of the book that she will not grow up too fast but will take things "one day at a time" (*Brave*, 130).

Readers curious about their developing bodies but lacking the words and self-assurance to question the adults in their lives about sex and sexuality can, by following Alice through her adventures, learn a great deal about their changing selves. Along with Alice, young readers can gather the knowledge they seek. One book at a time, they gain the understanding that builds the kind of self-esteem that Alice gradually acquires.

Being Friends

As Alice tries to stay on an even keel, balancing between Elizabeth the prudish and Pamela the advanced, she frequently has to consider the meaning of friendship. Naylor explores the trials and tribulations of adolescent female relationships with both tenderness and humor, and discloses the emotional seesaw that adolescents experience almost daily.

In the episode of the "Up-Lift Spandex Ahh-Bra," Pamela first brings the wonders of brassieres to the attention of Alice and Elizabeth. One summer evening, she is showing off her new find, describing the way the bra pushes up the breast so it sort of "puffs out over the top . . . 'A gentle assist for the undersized,' it read on the back of the tag. 'Lifts, supports, and promotes cleavage'" (*Rapture*, 53). While the girls are exploring the bra, their boyfriends come strolling by. Mark, who is going with Pamela, sneaks up, grabs the bra, runs off with it, puts it on, and climbs the jungle gym at the nearby playground. To his credit, he does not realize the bra belongs to his girlfriend—he thinks it is Elizabeth's. The bra is rescued, but Pamela is devastated.

> "Now everyone *knows*," Pamela wept when we got to the sidewalk.
> "Knows what?" I asked.
> "That I'm undersized!" Pamela wailed.
> "Everybody knew that before," Elizabeth said, trying to be helpful. It was not helpful. Pamela cried all the harder. (*Rapture*, 59)

Pamela plots revenge. She makes her friends promise that if they ever see Mark with spinach between his teeth they will not tell him. If they ever catch him with his zipper open, they must not tell him. Pamela wants her friends to maintain silence until he apologizes. Alice tells the reader, "I didn't promise that one right away because 'ever' is a long time. But when I thought about how awful Pamela had felt when he read the label on her bra, I knew I had to stick by her" (*Rapture*, 59).

Pamela also asks her friends to stop speaking to their boyfriends on the grounds that the other boys thought what Mark had done was funny. Now Alice gets herself into trouble.

> "Well, it *was* funny, Pamela, in a way," I said. Oh boy, was *that* ever the wrong thing to say.
> "Alice McKinley, you're not my friend either!" Pamela said. "And I don't think I'll ever speak to you until *you* apologize." (*Rapture*, 59)

The specific details Naylor employs—the name of the bra, the actual conversation, the strong verbs such as "wailed"—all serve to make the episode real, to infuse it with that memory of the "claustrophobic, self-absorbed agony" of adolescents so crucial to writing successfully for this age group. The tension Alice experiences as she negotiates between the loyalty she feels toward Pamela and that deserved by Patrick is familiar to every adolescent.

Although Alice usually tries to find a way to be a good friend (as in the "Ahh-bra" instance), in doing so she frequently finds herself in hot water. In *Reluctantly Alice* (1991; hereafter cited as *Reluctantly*), Elizabeth confides that she feels backward and immature because she has never seen a naked male body. Alice, wanting to be a real friend, decides to pore over every old issue of *National Geographic* for pictures of naked boys and men:

> There were about four hundred issues to go through, but I kept at it. Actually, there were only a few pictures of men from the front. Too many photographs had been taken from behind, or with the man holding a spear or shield right over the place Elizabeth most wanted to see. (*Reluctantly*, 86)

Lester wants to know what Alice is doing since she covers the entire dining room floor with her magazines. When she tells him the project is not for school but is for Elizabeth, he reaches out for the "best pictures" pile:

> I wriggled under the table on my stomach and buried my head in my arms . . . "I'll be a son of a gun," he said at last.
> I didn't want him making fun of Elizabeth. Not after all we'd shared and confided and promised. I sat up so fast I bumped my head on the table.
> "She's never seen a naked man in her life, and I'm just trying to help!" I bellowed. (*Reluctantly*, 88)

Fortunately, Alice's dad has entered the room. He tells her she can find the information she wants at the library and makes a date to take her there after school the next day. As is frequently the case, Mr. McKinley is an oasis of calm; his rational perspective teaches her that her curiosity is normal and natural, thus creating the safety and protection she needs to expand her horizons.

Alice often exhibits the same traits as her father when dealing with Pamela and Elizabeth. As the pragmatic member of the group and as a friend, she is the one who finds things out for all of them—like the fact that the library is a source of *that* kind of information. In *Alice In-Between*, however, Pamela tests the limits of their friendship and of Alice's ability to help during an

Amtrak journey to Chicago. The three girls are traveling together to visit Alice's Aunt Sally. Always ready for an adventure, Pamela, who is only 13, has done her best to look like a college student. She attracts the attention of 37-year-old Bill Donovan and agrees to have dinner with him, telling the others she just wants to have fun. Alice and Elizabeth stare at each other: "I think deep down we had known that someday this would happen; someday we would have to rescue Pamela" (*A in B*, 94).

After her dinner, Pamela rushes into the bedroom shared by Elizabeth and Alice appealing for help. The man had followed Pamela into her roomette and kissed her. "Suddenly Pamela was our friend again, a friend in need, and with her hair all wild and her lipstick half gone, she didn't look as old as she had, and I knew we would do whatever was necessary to save her" (*A in B*, 102). It is Alice who summons up the nerve to talk to Bill, who is drinking beer and searching for Pamela; she suggests he check the ladies' room or question the conductor. Continuing to take charge, she makes an "alarm" of shoe laces, nail clippers, a metal brush, and an aspirin bottle; she hangs this makeshift alarm on the door of the bedroom all three girls now occupy to warn them if Bill tries to get in while they are sleeping.

When Elizabeth cannot hold her tongue and tells Aunt Sally about Bill, it is Alice who manages to convince her aunt—and her father, notified by phone about the incident—that they really do know how to take care of themselves. Alice is also the one who realizes that Pamela has been very quiet all during their first day in Chicago. Attempting to draw Pamela out, she gets her to talk about the other things Bill tried to do, which leads Pamela to state that she does not believe in God:

> "The thing is," Pamela went on, "the Bible talks about all the miracles Jesus did. Why didn't he make Bill Donovan disappear? Why did all the good stuff take place back in the Bible, and now we just have their word for it?" (*A in B*, 11)

Alice knows how to help her companion find some sense of equilibrium again. She replies,

"I think it's sort of a miracle that we are sitting here talking like this—that we've finally made it through seventh grade. . . Can you imagine Brian and Patrick and Mark sitting under a tree talking about God?" (*A in B*, 117)

It is perhaps in *Alice in April* that Naylor most explicitly explores the nature of friendship. When Alice began seventh grade in *Reluctantly Alice*, she encountered Denise Whitlock, a bully who tormented her during "Seventh Grade Sing Day" and who made life miserable by teasing her about her mother's death. Alice managed to turn their relationship around by choosing to be Denise's partner for an interview project and by pointing out to Denise her positive qualities. In *Alice in April* the two girls are "more or less friends," and Alice begins to learn about Denise's very difficult home situation. Denise confesses that her mother does not like her and that the only time her mother ever gives her something is when she no longer wants it herself (*April*, 52). After that, Alice starts to realize that the various bruises and black eyes Denise frequently sports may be proof of these allegations. When Denise shows up in Language Arts with a black eye, Alice persuades her to talk about it and urges Denise to report her mother. Denise declines, saying it would not do any good; her mother is never going to change. Alice replies, "Some day she's going to feel really sorry she treated you like this" (*April*, 69).

Knowing Denise likes to hear about what is going on in Alice's family—"the way a dieter likes to hear about rich desserts" (*April*, 84)—Alice invites Denise to be a part of the surprise party she and Lester are planning for their dad's birthday. Denise begins to view Alice as a real friend. After another episode of abuse, she arrives on Alice's doorstep. Alice invites her in for dinner and, recognizing that Denise needs to feel safe and secure, invites her to stay all night. Alice falls asleep while Denise is telling her more about her life, but wakes up to the sound of Denise sobbing, and she begins to understand just how miserable Denise's life is.

Then comes the shocking news. An assembly is called at school the Monday after the surprise party. Denise had been at the party, helping out with the dishes, and had given Alice a bracelet, a picture of Tom Cruise, earrings, and a picture of herself from sixth grade. Alice thought Denise had had a good time, and she looks for her to thank her again for her help and for the presents. Instead, the principal makes an announcement to the student body. Recognizing that the students are hovering on the brink of adulthood and need to be treated with respect, he states that he will deliver some distressing news in as straightforward a manner as possible (like Naylor herself). He says, "I know that when you leave the gym today you will feel far older that you did when you came in. It is my painful task to tell you that one of our students, Denise Whitlock, was killed this morning when she apparently stood in the path of an oncoming train" (*April*, 155).

Alice berates herself for not having reported the abuse Denise suffered. She reproaches herself for not having recognized that the presents Denise gave her were a sign that she was thinking about the end, cleaning up her life. She feels guilty for never having truly *liked* Denise, even when she was being nice to the girl. Alice's dad points out that Alice did the best she could, and that Denise clearly valued her efforts because she chose Alice to receive her special treasures. At school the teachers try to help the students deal with the situation by talking about it; Pamela's mother makes enormous chocolate chunk cookies to help pull them through.

But Alice finds solace most readily through time spent with her friends. Each girl agrees to tell the others if she finds herself depressed enough to consider suicide. However, they also conclude that, as Pamela says, "When you come right down to it, all we can do is just try to be the best friends to each other that we can and hope it's enough" (*April*, 159). As Hazel Rochman writes in *ALA Booklist*, Naylor "is careful not to milk the situation, and though Alice grieves, her life goes on with all its daily trials and tribulations. . . . and whether the messages are about family, friendship, feminism, or sex, the tone is gentle; and people have a lot of fun, even if they don't live happily ever after."[5]

Being Part of a Couple
After Denise's suicide, Ben McKinley and Miss Summers—Alice's teacher—take a hot air balloon ride at sunrise, Lester's birthday

present to his father. Alice looks up at the two, their heads tilted back, laughing, and wonders if they will marry. Although her father has dated other women, she wants very much to have Miss Summers be a part of the family. Lester tells her not to interfere. Meanwhile, Lester's own love life becomes more and more complicated. In earlier books readers see Lester with Marilyn and Crystal and even Loretta, from the music store, who chases him. In this book, *Alice in April,* Lester invites a new woman, Joy, to the surprise birthday party for his dad. While Lester, according to Joy, makes eyes at his former girlfriends, she gets stuck talking to Loretta and becomes upset. Alice inquires about the state of Lester's relationships and learns that he is now back to talking on the phone with Marilyn and Crystal, and has sent Joy a rose, which appeases her, at least momentarily.

Naylor receives fan mail from adult women who read the Alice books in order to follow the love lives of the two McKinley men. But for adolescent readers and for Alice, the adult romances serve to demonstrate the various kinds of relationships men and women can have. As Alice tries to figure out what it means to be part of a couple, she watches her brother in action and talks to her father about his former marriage and about the current women in his life. These morsels of information provide a touchstone for Alice in her quest for understanding. One of the significant subplots running throughout the Alice books to date is that of the convolutions of Alice's relationship with Patrick. In general, Naylor provides a lovely model of how two young people can create a healthy companionship based on mutual respect, genuine caring for each other, and shared interests.

After the brief kiss between Alice and Patrick at the end of sixth grade (*The Agony of Alice,* 130), Naylor focuses on the developing relationship between them in *Alice in Rapture, Sort Of.* They try kissing again and Alice thinks about how delicious having a boyfriend is. On their second effort, they manage a real kiss. Patrick puts his arms around Alice and pulls her close: "It was so romantic my legs felt as though they were melting. I could feel my heart pounding, pounding beneath my checkered shirt. Your lips! Your arms! I wondered if *this* was how you felt when you said, 'I *want* you! I *need* you!'" (*Rapture*, 29). But pragmatic Alice then decides she will have to go through a lot of kisses before she ever can tell a boy something like that.

A review of *Alice in Rapture, Sort Of* in *Language Arts* notes the importance of such scenes as "rehearsal for young readers" struggling to make the leap from childhood friendship to adolescent romance.[6] As the summer unfolds, Alice and her readers find out there are a lot of rules about boy/girl interactions. She is told that girls do not call boys, that boys walk on the outside of the sidewalk, and that unless two people are married they cannot give each other gifts of clothing that touch the skin. Alice and Patrick muddle along, experimenting with French kissing. The first time, "the kiss went on so long, I wondered when I was allowed to swallow. What were the rules about that? Should the boy let you up for air every ten seconds, or were you supposed to sort of keep your nostrils to one side?" (*Rapture*, 83–84). Alice ends up bolting away from him, saying she is just not ready. Patrick looks relieved. Later they have their first argument, and in spite of how much she enjoys being recognized as part of a couple, Alice muses: "I wondered if maybe Patrick and I hadn't had more fun together back in the sixth grade when we were just eating lunch together, horsing around together at recess and sitting out on my porch talking. Before the kissing began" (*Rapture*, 89).

Alice finds love letters in the attic from her mother to her father, and, although feeling very guilty, she reads them. To her surprise, she sees the words, "I want you! I need you!" in a letter written just months before her parents married. Realizing that her mother was 11 years older at the point of writing those phrases than she is now, Alice is comforted to know she does not have to squeeze everything into a single summer. She decides to take her time with Patrick, and after a special dinner at his parents' club (more rules to follow about dining in elegance!), she asks if they can just be "special friends" because she realizes she is spending a lot of her time trying to determine just what Patrick thinks about her breath, her anatomy, her personality, her actions and mannerisms. She reflects on how much she likes him, realizing her feelings are more intense than Patrick probably knows, "but it was time to start liking myself, too. What did *I* think? What kind of person did *I* want to be? Something was missing here, and the something was me" (*Rapture*, 146).

Alice's decision seems natural and rings true. Consistent with the kind of advice her father both gives and follows himself, it is the kind of realistic attitude that caused Patrick to be attracted to Alice in the first place. Some reviewers find Patrick too sophisticated and mature for his age. True, he has a sense of self-confidence that allows him to treat others with respect. And he is a young man of integrity who is unlikely to confuse what he knows he should do with what others expect him to do—more so than some of his peers. For instance, when Alice confesses to Patrick that she cannot sing, he is determined to teach her. She protests, saying she does not want to look foolish in front of him. But Patrick looks her directly in the eye and tells her she can never look foolish in his eyes because he likes her too much: "Something warm and mushy filled my chest when he said that, and I believed him. . . . I knew that while he may have laughed at Mark Stedmeister wearing Pamela's bra, he wasn't going to laugh at me no matter how bad I sounded" (*Rapture*, 68).

But Patrick is, nonetheless, an adolescent boy. He is as eager to figure out kissing as is Alice. He does not understand how the girls feel when they learn they are being nicknamed by states. When Alice asks him to suggest a name to the boys involved, Patrick decides Maine would be good—not because of its topography but because he has gone fishing there with his father and just really likes the state. He can be awkward and say "dumb things." For instance, in *All But Alice* (1992; hereafter cited as *All But*), Patrick continues to work at being "special friends," giving Alice a box of chocolates for Valentine's Day. Practical Alice, who has just eaten two brownies, neglects to open the box and offer the candy to Patrick.

Of course she is chagrined to learn from Lester that when a boy gives a girl candy, it usually is because the *boy* wants some, too. Lester helps her out. She is to call Patrick and tell him the box had been too pretty to open, but now she is ready to do so and wants him to share the chocolates. Alice follows Lester's instructions, but Patrick says he wishes he had known she would not open the box right away "[b]ecause Valentine's candy is half-price now. I could have bought two boxes for what this one cost" (*All But*, 97). Alice says two boxes would make her fat. Patrick notes he had not said he would have given both boxes to *her*. Then, when she offers him the chance to take some home, he picks up a handful, decides he has taken too many, and puts several back in the box, complete with dents, and Alice is relieved to think that "Patrick the Perfect wasn't so perfect after all" (*All But*, 97).

On the other hand, Patrick has a matter-of-fact view of the world that frequently comes in handy when he needs to comfort Alice. When Lester and Alice have been arguing more than usual, in *Alice in April*, Alice ponders how she would feel if Lester died suddenly—perhaps by choking on a chicken bone—and her last words with him had been harsh ones. She imagines Lester's death so vividly that she begins sobbing in the hallway at school. She is crying so hard that all she can spit out when asked what is wrong is "It's Lester." Her friends assume he really *has* died, and take her to the nurse, who manages to calm her down. Her friends, knowing how embarrassed she must feel, keep assuring her she does not have to explain what happened, but Alice insists on setting the record straight. Patrick understands:

> Leave it to Patrick to break the ice. "I heard you flipped out at lunch today," he said, so everyone would hear. Of course everyone stopped talking and listened.
> "I didn't flip out. I was imagining how I'd feel if anything happened to Lester because I'd been so awful to him this week, and it almost seemed like something *had*, it got so real, even though I knew it hadn't."
> "Oh," said Patrick. And that's all there was to it (*April*, 59).

Alice does the same kind of thing for Patrick. In *All But Alice* Patrick was horribly embarrassed by throwing up—on some of his female peers. The boys in the in crowd decide to play a practical joke on him; Naylor shows her understanding of adolescent male humor having one of the boys describe this prank. As soon as Patrick gets on the bus, the girls are to scream, as if afraid he will upchuck on them again. Alice is to fake throwing up, and at that point, one of the boys will open his mouth and spit out a mixture of Cheerios and water (*All But*, 146).

At first Alice is tempted to participate. Having made a fool of herself at a talent show, she sees this as an opportunity to regain membership in the "Famous Eight," the "in" crowd. But she recalls how awful she felt during the talent show, and she is just too fond of Patrick to cause him that same humiliation. When he gets on the bus, she gets him to sit next to her and starts telling the story of Gounod's "Ave Maria," which she so thoroughly confused that Patrick remarks that she is *weird*. She does not care; all that matters is that she has rescued him. Feeling good about her choice, she lets him know she has kept special mementos of their relationship: the Valentine card he sent her in sixth grade, as well as the Milky Way wrapper from the candy bar he first threw at her.

Patrick's parents are most likely responsible for instilling so many positive traits in him. Alice learns that even though they are rich and have traveled all over the globe, they are genuinely nice people who are not stuffy or rigid. After eating dinner with his family on one occasion, Alice presents Patrick with a hermit crab as a birthday present. Expecting Mrs. Long to demand that Patrick remove it from the dining room, Alice is relieved when she exclaims instead, "A hermit crab! I haven't seen one of those in years. What a marvelous present, Alice" (*A in B*, 130). She is delighted when Patrick puts the crab right on the dining room table among the various serving bowls, making everyone laugh.

At the end of *Alice In-Between*, after Alice and Patrick have created a new home for the hermit crab, talked about her trip to Chicago, and played on Patrick's new drum set, Patrick walks Alice home. It is a beautiful night; they are strolling along companionably. Given all that has passed in the Alice books up to this point, all the times they have come to each other's aid, all the advice and help they have given to each other, it is no real surprise that their relationship is ready for another turn. Patrick reaches over, puts his arm around Alice, and pulls her close. When they reach her door, they kiss. It feels right, comfortable and cozy, a kiss prompted out of something more than just hormones raging or a need to keep up with the "in" crowd. Readers grin along with Alice when she tells her father, "I am wonderful . . . positively wonderful" (*A in B*, 135).

Dealing with Family Ties

Alice's father is a good role model for being a part of a couple. When the "Alice" series begins, Ben McKinley, a widower of seven years and responsible for raising two children, has not taken the plunge into dating. Naylor develops Ben as she moves Alice forward in relationships, using his and Lester's interactions with women to provide appealing counterpoint to Alice's feelings about Patrick.

Having decided her father should marry her seventh-grade English teacher, Miss Summers, Alice finagles a meeting between the two. With her dad's permission to invite someone to attend a performance of the *Messiah*, she asks Miss Summers to go and surprises them both when it is time to drive to the concert. Comfortable conversation and a shared passion for music provide the basis for a budding romance, underscoring Alice's own developing awareness that she and Patrick have something more valuable than Pamela and her boyfriends, selected mostly for their good looks.

In *Alice the Brave*, Ben volunteers to take Alice, Pamela, and Elizabeth camping—and Miss Summers. The impending trip occasions a frank discussion between Alice and her dad about sex. Alice wants to know where Miss Summers will sleep. She states, "If you'd just come right out and say whether or not you're having sex with her, then people could think about other things" (*Brave*, 42). Ben wonders why nobody cares whether or not they have interesting conversations, asking, "Why is it that the only thing that interests other people is whether or not we're having sex?" Alice thinks about that question and replies,

> I guess it's because sex is one of the few things you do in private, so that's what everyone is curious about. And maybe they think that if two people are having sex, they've already *had* interesting conversations. (*Brave*, 49)

Lester jumps into the discussion, noting that lots of guys of his acquaintance sleep with girls and do not even know their names. Ben says, "That's what I'm talking about!"

After the camping trip, Alice notes that her dad and Miss Summers seem more distant toward each other, and this observation prompts her to ask him whether people happily married can still be attracted to somebody else. Once again, her father is honest and direct, observing that this happens all the time. Alice asks if it ever happened to him when her mother was alive. His "[s]ure" upsets her equilibrium: "The warm little bubble I'd carried around with me ever since I can remember seemed to have been popped by a cold wind" (*Brave*, 123). But her father is able to teach her more about marriage by his response:

> Listen, sweetheart, I dated six women before I met your mother, and there were probably two billion women in the world at that particular time. Just looking at it mathematically, there were probably a million I might have been happier with or who suited me better than Marie. . . . Why did I marry her? Because I knew that she was a woman I could love—that I *did* love. And since I couldn't possibly date all the other women I'd be meeting in my lifetime, why not settle on her? I was committed to the marriage, Al. That's what makes the difference." (*Brave*, 123)

Ben's words likely have an effect on Alice in part because she has witnessed Lester's seesaw relationships with Crystal and Marilyn. Lester frequently tells her why he likes both for different reasons, values each in unique ways, and cannot make up his mind about making an exclusive commitment to either of them. No wonder Alice takes things slowly with Patrick and values their easy, companionable friendship as much as the romantic aspects of their relationship.

One of the other hallmarks of Alice's progress toward maturity is that her relationship with her brother deepens over time. When readers first meet them, Alice is 11 and Lester is 19, and, for the most part, they pick on each other and play practical jokes. In time, Alice is able to recognize when Lester is hurting and does her best to comfort him and to respond empathetically. At the same time, Lester finds ways to guide Alice through some of the agonies of puberty. In *Alice the Brave,* when his nose tells him it is time for Alice to begin using deodorant, he handles the situation with great tact: Poking his head in her door, he shouts "Hey, Al! Present! Catch!" and tosses her a Lady Mennen. Later, in the same book, Naylor discloses just how lucky Alice is to have Lester for an older brother when he teaches her—successfully and tenderly—to overcome her fear of deep water. In Alice's family, no matter how much the three of them may bicker, no matter how much they may tease, when the chips are down, they come to each other's rescue.

In each book, Alice also learns more about her mother and, in the process, more about herself and her family. In *Alice in Rapture, Sort Of*, Alice finds her mother's and father's love letters from their courting days. When planning a surprise birthday party for her father in *Alice In April*, she finds a recipe for pineapple upside-down cake—in her mother's writing and labeled "Ben's favorite"—stuffed in the recipe box. In *Alice the Brave,* part of Alice's motivation for finally learning to swim derives from discovering that her mother loved the sport and from hearing her father mistakenly tell her she resembles her mother in that respect. She starts to feel good about her hair when Lester mentions that its unique strawberry blonde color comes from her mother. Unearthing more about her parents' marriage from her father, Alice comes to feel her mother's presence guiding her into young womanhood.

Creating "Alice McKinley"

What are the origins of Alice McKinley? According to Naylor, Alice and her friends have their roots in their creator's own girlhood. Speaking at the 1992 Workshop of the Adolescent Literature Assembly of the National Council of Teachers of English, Naylor outlined those traits that she and Alice share, although aware that her youth was very different from adolescent life today. For instance, some of her fondest memories are of bedtimes in summer. She would giggle with her older sister Norma in a double bed, the sheet pulled up over their heads, while their father walked through the room spraying a mosquito repellent. Waiting for sleep to arrive, they would tap out rhythms of popular songs on the wall for each other and guess what tune was being "played."[7] Patrick and Chris (from *A String of Chances*) are both gifted drummers, and Alice herself sounds out rhythms accurately. Naylor, however, doubts today's youth experience bedtime in the same way she did as an adolescent.

Naylor also vividly recalls participating in air raid drills and blackouts during World War II; these kinds of experiences, she realizes, are not all that relevant to today's youth. Naylor "brings instead the feelings I remember so well" to bear on her novels for young adults: the embarrassment of comparing her body's development to that of others, the tensions that arise when adolescents try to separate themselves from their parents' identities. She states,

> For those who write YA fiction, it is our willingness to step back into that claustrophobic, self-absorbed agony of adolescence that enables us—demands of us—to put those feelings down on paper so that other young people will know that others have walked these paths and lived to tell about it.[8]

In many ways, Alice is a reincarnation of Naylor herself. Adolescent psychologist David Elkind in *All Grown Up and No Place to Go* describes the "imaginary audience" phenomenon as the belief that everyone else in one's world can recall all the tiny details of each stupid, embarrassing incident in which one has ever been involved.[9] The thought processes of adolescents have matured enough to allow them to visualize possible futures, but adolescents retain much of the egocentrism of childhood. Hence, they often spend a great deal of time agonizing over their performances, imagining how they looked and seemed to others.

Many of the specifics of Alice's concern with her "imaginary audience" and others' perception of her actions come directly from Naylor's life. For example, one of the "agonies" Alice relives at the beginning of *The Agony of Alice* involves a boy, Donald Sheavers, a big piece of cardboard from the Sears washing machine box, and Tarzan movies. Alice wants to use the cardboard as a raft and to act out a scene from a Tarzan movie in which Tarzan and Jane kiss while floating down the river. They reenact all the action leading up to the kiss but never actually do the deed.

The entire Tarzan situation resembles one Naylor lived through. She uses it well at the beginning of *The Agony of Alice* to provide a contrast with the first kiss scene between Alice and Patrick and to show how the young people mature. Naylor says that, in general, the reason for doing the series at all was "to show growth over time."[10]

In addition, Alice, like Naylor, is a worrier who usually attempts to do something concrete about difficult situations. Naylor, growing up during World War II, recalls worrying about the Nazis, living in fear they would march into the Reynolds household, and take their food. As a small girl, Naylor stuffed bread into their pencil sharpener so that her family would have something to sustain them in the event of a Nazi invasion. Her somewhat misguided efforts resemble those of Alice trying to help Elizabeth by searching through *National Geographic* magazines for pictures of the male body.[11]

The character of Elizabeth is based on a friend from Naylor's own youth as well. Naylor recalls being 16 and in a car with several other girls—no adults—driving to a summer cottage for a weekend. Feeling very grown up and excited, they rolled down the windows and began singing a racy song. One of the young women insisted that if their singing did not cease immediately, she was getting out of the car and hitchhiking home. Naylor says, "We stopped. It was her parents' cottage, after all." Later, at bedtime in the cottage, the conversation turned to the wedding night. They were having a marvelous time trying to figure out what it would be like, but the same young woman demanded that they stop their talk or she would go home.[12] Now, whenever Elizabeth makes an appearance in one of the Alice books, Naylor wonders where that friend is and what she is doing. Naylor says Alice asks a lot of the questions she herself never felt comfortable asking—and the adults in Alice's life provide the concrete, matter-of-fact replies Naylor always wanted.

The Alice books are also the product of Naylor's 20-some years of writing prior to the publication of *The Agony of Alice* in 1985. The ability to create believable brother/sister dialogue between Lester and Alice was honed in the Tedesco column, *In Small Doses*, and other earlier works. Their interactions, their ability both to show affection—but only in understated ways—and to annoy each other closely resemble those of Tedesco and his sister Kate.

Naylor even uses similar incidents in more than one book, developing their power over time. As noted earlier, Alice quarrels with Lester at one point and frets about the incident afterward. By vividly imagining that he has died, she works herself into a tizzy and has to go to the school nurse. Becky, in the "Late Brennan Brothers," a story in *Never Born a Hero* (1982), applies the same strategy to the point "where all Jason or Fred [her brothers] had to do was walk into the room and Becky's eyes would grow misty."[13] This same situation is repeated in *The Year of the Gopher* before it appears in the 1993 *Alice in April*.

Perhaps Ben McKinley is as understanding and honest a father as he is because Naylor had already created several similarly down-to-earth fathers in earlier novels. In the "Witch" series, for instance, begun in 1975, it is Lynn's father who takes Lynn seriously as she voices her fears about the presence of witchcraft in her life. Further, in the very early *When Rivers Meet*, the father treats his children with respect, trusting their judgment, and supporting them when the community finds their lack of racial prejudice offensive.

Responding to "Alice"

Thus the Alice books reveal the maturing process of both Naylor the writer and Alice the young girl. As Alice advances through the sixth, seventh, and eighth grades, she becomes a young woman who learns to make peace with her body and to think for herself. At the same time, Naylor sharpens her ability to construct a tight plot, to weave serious issues into basically very funny books, to capture adolescent dialogue, and to deepen her characterizations of those who people Alice's world. By the time *Alice In-Between* was published, reviewers had come to expect excellence, and they praised Naylor's aptitude for creating a "droll tale of early adolescent pluck, curiosity, and angst."[14] In *Horn Book* Naylor's good plotting and effective dialogue in this book are also noted as strengths.[15] Terms like "hilarious,"[16] "plenty of laughs,"[17] and "amusing and insightful"[18] are routinely used by reviewers in describing the appeal of the Alice books. Naylor's use of vivid detail contributes to the poignant humor of the series, for which she is also consistently praised.

Many authors who write for young adults find favor with the reviewers, so perhaps it is most fitting to allow an adolescent female, a real-life "Alice," describe the contributions of the Alice books to the field of young adult literature. During the ALAN workshop talk in November of 1992, Naylor quoted a letter written to her by a young girl from Vancouver—an adolescent herself—who articulates the reasons the Alice books are so powerfully appealing:

> I am not the kind of person who likes books about old times or about the future, but prefers modern, interesting books that are humorous. Unfortunately, these are the hardest books in the world to find. But I absolutely love the "Alice" books so much that you are right up there at the top with my favorite authors. If you should ask me why, then here's my answer. From Patrick to Elizabeth to Pamela to Ocean City to the "Aah-bra" to Mark and Tom to Little Jimmy and the grape stuck in his throat and Mrs. Plotkin in her green dress to the summer of the first boyfriend to "SGSD" . . . to Miss Summers and Miss Cole and the real life drama of not having a mother, to Lester and Marilyn and Crystal, and many more things, your books have warmed my heart. . . . Sometimes I'm sad that Alice isn't real. Or is she? I hope you understand how much I congratulate you

on your skill. I used to love Betsy books and Ramona books, but I grew up faster than they did, and now cannot enjoy those books because I am too old and kind of in a different stage of life than them. But please don't let this happen to Alice. It would mean a whole world to me.[19]

3. On Surviving One's Family: The "York Trilogy," *The Solomon System, The Keeper,* and *Crazy Love*

Naylor believes in the importance of offering her readers humorous books like the "Alice" series. Reading such books, she notes, provides young adults with a way to escape from the difficulties of day-to-day existence. However, Naylor also says she will go on writing books about serious subjects because they are a part of life and "facing them is a part of growing up."[1] Coping with the pressures and conflicts arising from the adolescent's effort to find his or her place both within the family and outside its boundaries is a major theme of much of Naylor's work for older teenagers.

As her own sons became young men during turbulent times on the international scene, Naylor began to witness the effects that uncertainty and difficult circumstances have on an adolescent's view of the future. She also witnessed the tight control that many parents exert over their child's life. With little regard for their child's sense of self or notions of life's possibilities, they busily organize the present and outline the future. Naylor's efforts to help young people cope with family instability is the subject of this chapter; her books about adolescents struggling to develop an independence from their families is the focus of chapter 4.

The "York Trilogy" Novels
and the Metaphor of Disease

The "York Trilogy" books exhibit Naylor's desire to help young adults acknowledge and accept the contingencies of life and advance purposefully into the future. In the late 1970s, Naylor had two experiences that led her to write these three books. She was reading *The Washington Post* travel section and ran across an article about the most recent sighting of the ghosts of Roman soldiers often reportedly encountered in the cellar of the Treasurer's House in York, England. She was immediately attracted to this story and told her husband, "I've got to go. I've just got to go. I'm so drawn by this story." She wanted to visit York, to find out about the ghosts, and to learn about the personalities of those who claimed to have met them. At the same time, her own sons were apprehensive about the future of the planet because of the constant threat of nuclear war. Naylor wondered what she could do to provide an optimistic sense of the future for them when she herself felt anxious about it. The result was an allegory about historical York that was designed to

> show my own sons and other young people that there have been other times ... when people were terribly afraid in different ways, when savagery was directed at individuals, and each person could be hunted down, plus the Black Plague—no one knew what caused it, how to stop it, and everyone was frightened.

She hoped that reading about Dan—high school student and main character of these books—and his travels into the past would reassure adolescents that they are not alone in sensing an unpredictable future. At the beginning of *Faces in the Water* (1981; hereafter cited as *Faces*), she quotes Marcus Aurelius Antoninus in order to illustrate her position. She wants young people to recognize "the universe is change; our life is what our thoughts make it." No matter what the time period, the possibility for total annihilation—of people, works of art, books, and everything we hold dear—exists. Thus the first volume, *Shadows on the Wall* (1980; hereafter cited as *Shadows*), begins with a description of how the waters of the earth intertwine the past, present, and future:

> Never since the world began has a single drop of water been added to the earth, nor a single drop taken away. The cup of water in your hand may have passed through the lips of Constantine the Great or Attila the Hun. The water in which you bathe may have washed the face of hero and villain alike.
>
> There are those who believe that some Primitive Unknown passes from spring to brook to river and sea, making all waters one, a quivering repository of collective being—that it is in the waters of the earth that life flows on, linking the past to future. (*Shadows*, 3)

Simultaneously, Naylor was researching an article for a church paper. She had heard about the "normal volunteers" at the National Institutes for Health (NIH)—young people who volunteered to be the controls in experiments, getting paid perhaps five dollars a day for three weeks to live on a diet of rice and egg whites or to sit in a cold room with their feet in cold water. Naylor was so impressed with the implied altruism of these young people that she went to NIH to interview some of them for an article on "How to Spend Your Summer Vacation." She asked one of the volunteers what the hardest part of his job had been. He said he had had difficulty visiting a patient with Huntington's disease and seeing the patient's two teenaged daughters in the room, girls about his own age who knew that they had a 50 percent chance of developing the disease themselves. Naylor states,

> That really stuck with me. I thought, "That must be one of the worst things to go through. You can't plan your life. You don't know whether to marry or have children. If you do have the gene, it may not show up until you're 45, or even 65 in some cases." So I thought I would use this situation throughout the trilogy; Dan would have this possibility to face.

At the time that Naylor wrote the York books, there was no medical test to determine whether a specific individual was carrying the gene for Huntington's disease. A defect in this gene destroys nerve cells in the brain, causing symptoms that mimic alcoholism and mental illness. Most people with whom Naylor spoke at that time told her they wanted an infallible way to know what the future held in store. Now that such a test does exist, however, many individuals choose not to take it, a fact Naylor finds intriguing. She maintains that she herself would probably choose not to know the outcome of such a test. She reasons that, in the event of a positive result, she would lose hope in the future, and that would be devastating. Coming of age when the test was unavailable, Dan has to find a way to think hopefully about the future and create a sense of optimism in the face of uncertainty.

At first Dan explores relics of the past that exist in contemporary York, having traveled there with his parents. His mission: to write about ancient times for his school newspaper. In addition, he desperately wants to ferret out the real reasons his parents have brought him to the city. Eventually they tell him that they are trying to track down records of Dan's father's relatives, whose behavior during their lifetime was apparently consistent with the presence of Huntington's. In this book, before traveling back in time to the days of Roman York, Dan wonders,

> How did you go about arranging your life with something hanging over your head all the time? How did you make yourself cram through four years of college? . . . How did you even think about having a wife, a family, knowing that you might be passing the defect on to your children before it was discovered in yourself? (*Shadows*, 4)

Dan's history teacher quotes Manilius, a Roman politician whose words jolt him: "As soon as we are born, we begin to die, and the end depends upon the beginning."

Dan is then drawn into the past as he becomes a time traveler— able to move back and forth between the present and ancient times. He sees the "shadows on the wall" of ancient Roman soldiers who seem to want him to join their ranks. He is torn. Should he confront these enemies, soldiers who want to tear him away from what is familiar? Or should he give in, become one of them, and live a secure life in which someone else would dictate all his movements? The centurions march past him, heading off to battle, and Dan is overwhelmed by the momentousness of the situation:

> Terror clutched at him, and yet, inside himself, he realized a fear even more deadly for he sensed that some part of him wished to go. Some part of him craved an end to uncertainty, with no price too high for the relief of it. . . . If he went, he would become one with the past, with the future decided for him. . . . In opting for security, he would lose forever the hope of change. (*Shadows*, 129)

Dan decides to resist the temptation to become a soldier. As a counterpoint to Dan, Naylor offers the reader Ambrose—gypsy and strong-willed leader of a Romany clan—who values tradition because it makes his position secure. Ambrose's lifestyle is continuously threatened by the increasingly technological and crowded nature of modern society: "[T]he more unrewarding the present, the more uncertain the future, the more he turned to the past" (*Shadows*, 140). Ambrose's point of view, however, is counterbalanced by that of Rose Faw, a gypsy woman who advises Dan, "Feed tomorrow and it will eat the joy of today" (*Shadows*, 160). After his experiences with the soldiers of long ago and the contemporary gypsy family, Dan decides that he does not want the future to dictate how he lives in the present.

However, actually carrying out his life based on that conclusion promises to be more difficult than reaching the insight was. When we meet Dan again in *Faces in the Water*, he is depressed and angry about the turn of events in his life. As she did in the first York book, Naylor uses the analogy of water (a river this time) to provide a conceptual framework for the reader who, along with Dan, is struggling to comprehend the fact that life is seldom predictable. This volume opens with a prologue describing the Susquehanna River, along whose banks the second act of Dan's adventures takes place. The prologue demonstrates Naylor's ability to match the cadence and rhythm of her language to the images and message her words convey. She then notes that in

1630 a shipyard owner and hotel proprietor from Colchester, England, migrated to America. Nathaniel Wells carried with him the gene for Huntington's disease, as did three other men, who, together, were responsible for the spread of the disease throughout the New World. Their genetic legacy—and the hidden nature of Dan's history—is described as analogous to the river's: Beneath the currents of its waters, there are "currents that travel unrecognized channels from ancient generations to our own" (*Faces*, ii). As his grandmother, Bee, says,

> You see, Dan, everything begins and ends in water. That's what my mother used to tell me. . . . She always said that when you dip your hand into a river, you drink a little of what you were and what you're yet to be. (*Faces*, 44–45)

Bee accepts herself and the terms that life has offered her; she also understands that time ebbs and flows like a river. At first Dan finds her outlook untenable—but deep down he knows he must adopt Bee's attitude for himself.

In *Faces,* at the "edge of dawn" (symbolizing the edge of the future), Dan repeatedly hears someone or something calling his name. Just as he wishes to ignore the potential for Huntington's in his future, he attempts to ignore this voice, Shortly thereafter, when he is in the basement—a space under Bee's house that shelters a pool, a sort of spring—he sees in the water the face of Orlenda, a gypsy girl from the first book with whom he was half in love, both in the present time and in their Roman incarnations. When Dan acts on his very real and honest feelings for this girl, stepping outside his own concerns, he is able to move through time, a journey Naylor describes poetically, capturing the rhythm of time and life itself in the process:

> He did not know how he got outside—only that he was drenched, as though he had fallen headfirst into a river. He almost remembered the falling itself—leaning forward, tipping, then down, down, sucked in by a current more powerful than he had ever dreamed, through tunnels of rock and tunnels of time, through light and dark, birth and death and oceans and oceans

around him. As though he had aged and been reborn again and again, but here he was, outside the house, trembling with cold. (*Faces*, 60)

Shivering and aware of his body once again, he realizes that his clothes have been transformed and that his grandmother's house is no longer in sight; another dwelling stands on its spot. He has landed in the backyard of Orlenda's family, who are terrified of the Romans. Centered in York, the Romans have been warring throughout the countryside, adding ever more land to their empire. Ambrose, father of the clan, has organized an underground rebellion, but Dan—despite his lack of support of the Roman operation—does not want to fight. He wonders,

> Yet the Romans—what was it to them that land and still more land should be added to the empire? How many acres were worth a man's life? To the man who gave it, was the reward ever large enough? Who decided that a man should fight? (*Faces*, 93)

In *Faces in the Water*, more so than in *Shadows*, Naylor allows various characters to present a pacifist point of view. As a mother of two young men coming of age in a world torn by civil and international strife, she was concerned about how parents could help their children confront the nature of barbarism. Through Dan's story, Naylor asks readers to consider whether it makes sense to resort to brutality in order to prevent it. Dan is not the only character to puzzle over the reasons for the war in which he has found himself embroiled. Back in the present, Bee makes a speech decrying the fact that the U.S. government spends millions of dollars on weapons research and on maintenance of the war machine, yet fails to fund scientific research to the same extent. Rose Faw, the mother of Orlenda, voices the concern of mothers throughout time faced with the possibility that their sons may have to march off to war: "And who's to protect us from our protectors? . . . War is war, whether the army is splendid or desperate. It is madness no matter who wins" (*Faces*, 68).

Dan decides to help the Faw family by scouting out the dangers of the road from their village to York. He is caught by a Roman soldier patrolling the road and is coerced, on threat of his life, into carrying a message to the city. While Dan is carrying out this task, Ambrose and followers attack him and find tangible evidence of his apparent collusion with the Romans in his possession. Assuming, of course, that he is a traitor, they tie him up, leaving him to die. At that point, Dan experiences the first breakthrough in his emotional stalemate over the Huntington's issue. He decides he does not want to end his life "betwixt and between." Realizing that vacillation has caused civilizations to crumble, he wants to be able to say he himself has taken a positive stand. He wonders,

> What if everyone took his position? What if no one fought for any cause whatsoever? ... It was not an argument easily answered. There was no glory in refusing to go, no trumpets or banners for the men who stayed behind. Yet there was something deeper and that was conscience.... If civilization depended on mass murder to save it, was it worth the price? (*Faces*, 99–100)

Freed by another member of Ambrose's family, he vows to help Orlenda and her siblings search out a new life and to work against the Romans. Having made that decision, Dan is filled with a rage to live. He knows he may never see Orlenda again, and he knows he can control neither her future nor his own. But he *can* control the present by taking decisive action on her behalf that might have a ripple effect long after they separate.

When Dan returns to the present, that rage to live stays with him, a passion born of reaching out to others, of recognizing the interconnectedness of individual lives in a much larger scheme. For his grandmother he makes the analogy between his mindset before his time travels and the paralysis felt by people during the height of the Bubonic Plague. He promises not to let fear of Huntington's paralyze him in the same way.

In *Footprints at the Window*, Dan's analogy with the Plague years becomes the reality through which he learns even more about the nature of caring and of taking positive action for the general good as antidotes to the paralysis of fear. At the end of

Faces in the Water, Naylor once more uses powerful descriptive language to indicate the intensity of the fear that Dan faces. Although he has decided to take action, he little realizes the almost deadly consequences of confrontation. Ambrose the gypsy attacked Dan not only in Roman times but also in present-day York, where Ambrose has been a menacing force in Dan's life. Dan decides to peer into Bee's basement pool and challenge Ambrose to show himself and resolve their quarrel. By describing the way Dan's skin prickles as the wind rushes through the basement wall where the stream enters, Naylor lets the reader know that something momentous may be about to happen. "The gentle bubbling sound of the water became more like a crackle, like dry branches giving way under footsteps, and the entire cellar grew darker still in the gloom of the afternoon" (*Faces*, 158).

Ambrose refuses to materialize; his face fades from sight, and the reader realizes that Dan will have to confront situations worse than those he has already survived before he is able to create a positive "now" for himself.

When Naylor describes the unstoppable tide of the Black Death flowing toward York in the prologue of the third book, the reader feels Dan's terror. Returning to the past, Dan confronts the Plague and overcomes that terror. In contrast, in scenes set in Dan's present, Naylor extends the analogy of the Plague years not only to the uncertainty of Huntington's but also to the insecurity spawned by the Cold War—of living life in the shadow of the atomic bomb.

Naylor introduces Dan's friend Bill in this novel. Editor of the school newspaper, Bill realizes that summer is drawing to a close and Dan has yet to turn in the promised feature on his spring trip to York. Upset, Bill arrives at Bee's house. Dan, now more willing to open himself up to others, tells Bill about his father's situation. Trying to empathize, Bill accepts Dan's fears as real and describes how his own obsession with the bomb makes him almost "want to puke" (*Footprints*, 28). Like Bee in *Faces*, Bill argues that the government should stop funding its gigantic war machine so generously and instead put money into medical research. Like many adolescents, however, Bill can see both sides of the argument. He appreciates his uncle's claim that more weapons of all kinds and more troops may keep the country strong and so maintain the peace. At the same time he recognizes the validity of his father's position, which is that continuing to build up the country's defenses merely keeps the arms race escalating, hastening the day when battle will be done (*Footprints*, 29). He wonders who is right and who is wrong.

After a good deal of consideration, however, Bill finds his own position. Rather than be torn apart by the irreconcilable differences between the adults in his life, Bill yearns to break free of the boundaries created by posing false alternatives, a lesson Dan is learning. Bill says we need a new Columbus, someone who can conceptualize options:

> And today, we still think in terms of war or surrender. If you can't work things out at the conference table, you fight. If you're not top dog, number one, you're going to end up slaves. People just accept that this is true. I don't think it is. We need a new explorer to come up with alternatives; that's where Columbus comes in. (*Footprints*, 34)

Bill has decided that even as an unempowered adolescent, he can use his talents as a writer and his position as school newspaper editor to advantage. He writes about world issues, exploring both sides of arguments and voicing his own opinions. Knowing he is trying to make the present and the future better enables him to enjoy life: "At least I'll know I was one of the ones who tried; that's what keeps me going" (*Footprints*, 34). Interestingly, Naylor found herself in Bill's position just a few years later—in (1984)—writing *The Dark of the Tunnel*. The book protested the inanities of the civil defense drill procedures instituted by a government that was heedless of the implications of their mandates. The Ambrose Faw family, so much a part of Dan's previous adventures, is not present in *Footprints* but they have close counterparts. Another gypsy family enters the picture, camping along the river near Dan's grandmother's house, and he is drawn to them. He makes a connection with Oriole, the daughter, who reminds him greatly of Orlenda from previous books. Oriole tells him about her family's actions on behalf of her brother, Gabe, who has gone AWOL from the army. Again, the pacifist message is entwined around the plot. Gabe has run away from his sergeant and the chaplain who have tried to convince him to hate the abstract "enemy" and to view killing one's fellow man as a "horrible necessity." Oriole tells Dan,

> You have to hate someone you don't even know. Someone that—if there weren't a war—you might like to walk beside in the woods, or fish beside in the streams or sit beside when you play your guitar. . . . That is the worst evil of all, doing awful things pretending all the while you are really brave and good. How much simpler it is when conscience and duty agree. (*Footprints*, 56–57)

Thus, the York books echo the beliefs of many young people coming of age in the post-Vietnam era. Enraged by the difficulties in determining the "good guys" from the "bad guys" in Vietnam, they were aware that such conflicts were likely to erupt in ever increasing numbers as population explodes and the world reaches the limits of its ability to sustain itself. Although Naylor has no concrete solution to offer, in Dan, in Bill, in Bee, and eventually in Dan's father, she provides models of the kind of thinking required for real change and a better tomorrow by every player in life's game of chance. At the end of *Footprints*, Dan of the Plague years succeeds in securing a horse, required by Orlenda's family if they are to escape the plague-infested environs of York. But only Orlenda and her younger siblings, Rachel and Nat, can leave; the horse can carry only so many pounds; thus Dan cannot go with them. He realizes he may never see the young woman and her siblings again, but despite a deep, sharp sadness, he is quite puzzled to realize that he is also experiencing something he can identify only as joy:

> *How could this be?* He asked himself. . . . How could he even persuade himself that he had saved Orlenda's life when she could fall ill tomorrow or the day after that and die without his even knowing? . . .

> He examined his joy. . . . He was living under a risk, but this
> itself made his life more precious, his accomplishments more
> meaningful, even if no one else knew it but he. It was indeed
> possible, he decided, for a person living under such odds, such
> uncertainties, to live his life well, regardless of how much time
> he was given. (*Footprints*, 130–31)

What a miracle it was that he—or anyone else—had been born at all, he mused. He had been one of four hundred million spermatozoa, all racing for the ovum, but he was the one who had made it. He lived. Even if he accomplished nothing, his life was a miracle. All life was a miracle, and those who spent their years never knowing that were the ones who missed out. (*Footprints*, 131–32)

The image of the lucky sperm is one Naylor has several of her characters—from a young man in a very early short story to George in *The Year of the Gopher*—share as a way of making concrete the knowledge of their uniqueness and of the miracle of life.

Dan returns to the present able to discuss the situation with his father for the first time in months. Dan acknowledges that he has been acting as if he were entitled to a guaranteed full life span. Now he and his father both comprehend that the Huntington's problem is not the only uncertainty they will ever face, and they are able to plan for the future in spite of the acceptance of their own mortality. Dan has learned that having true courage means living with hope.

Critics praised the York books for their realistic portrayal of events and for the "gripping intensity" of Naylor's descriptions of Dan and his fears.[2] Her skill in creating a time travel/adventure fantasy within a strong plot line carried out over the three volumes, and in interweaving metaphysical questions of grave significance to young adults is frequently noted by reviewers of prestigious journals such as *School Library Journal*,[3] *Horn Book*,[4] *Publishers Weekly*,[5] and *Booklist*.[6] The *Booklist* reviewer commends her as well for a writing style characterized by "vitality and assurance." Her use of analogy, her descriptive prowess, and her ability to foreshadow future events in intriguing ways all contribute to the success of this very tightly executed series.

The Solomon System and
Facing Changes in the Family Structure

Change and uncertainty in the wake of their parents' impending divorce—and how to retain a sense of hope—are the major hurdles facing Ted and Nory in *The Solomon System* (1983; hereafter cited as *Solomon*). Ted, the younger brother, is especially hard hit by the divorce's disruption of normal family life. For years he has believed in the "Solomon System," the term the brothers use to describe their belief that they can tackle new situations, accomplish difficult tasks, and face the world on optimistic terms. But, at 16, Nory is beginning to desire the separation from family that is a normal part of the search for an independent identity. At the summer camp they have always attended, Nory pulls away from Ted, both physically and emotionally, and both boys are, therefore, left alone to cope with the anxiety and grief they feel about their parents' tensions.

Although the tone of *The Solomon System* is basically serious, Naylor interjects some of the humor that she uses so effectively to make Alice and her friends sympathetic and real. At one point, Ted, the narrator, describes his brother Nory's concern about getting body hair:

> Nory, my brother, worries about body hair. He'll be sixteen next month, and he has hardly any hair on his legs. He says if he doesn't get hair on his chest he can live with it, but if he doesn't get hair on his legs he'll kill himself. (*Solomon*, 4)

Before the status quo is shattered by their parents' news of imminent divorce, Naylor uses such descriptions of the boys' concerns and their relationship early in the novel to demonstrate how normal they are.

At the same time, Naylor is establishing the tension in Ted's house, and the reader begins to recognize the limitations of his perspective. Ted tells us, for instance, about the routine of dinner table conversation, in which each boy receives a question in rotation; as soon as one of them answers his question, the other one is tossed a query. Ted realizes something is wrong; he tells the reader, "I guess our parents figured that as long as they're talking to us they don't have to talk to each other" (*Solomon*, 5). But Ted buys into the charade, saying sometimes he even tries to plan a story as soon as he gets up in the morning, one designed to make everyone laugh, so that he can feel a sense of family unity that otherwise is missing. A review in The *Horn Book* noted Naylor's ability to capture the dialogue of young people, to paint a vivid picture of camp life, and to leaven "an essentially serious story with humor and vivacity."[7]

Eventually, even Ted has to face facts. His mother says that the only thing she and his father have in common is that they are parents of the same two boys. Ted's sense of responsibility suddenly increases dramatically:

> That *really* scared me. . . . The one thing worse than feeling you can't do anything is the feeling that it's all up to you: you're responsible. (*Solomon*, 20)

Ted is not sure he wants to go away to camp this year, a camp he has always attended, feeling that without his presence as "glue," his parents will, in fact, split. He does not deal well with the lack of direction and definition in his family life, noting, rather like Dan from the York books,

> I have to know where things are headed. I'm the one who watches the road map when we go on a trip while everyone else looks out the windows. I like to say, 'Huntsville coming up, Dad, in exactly two and a half miles' and then see the sign for Huntsville. But suddenly, here we were, on a trip without a map. (*Solomon*, 21)

Still, it is Ted, rather than the older Nory, who more readily discovers coping mechanisms that facilitate the journey "without a map." After telling friends at camp that his parents are splitting up, he feels a sense of relief and a dissipation of some of his anger. Nory refuses to talk about the situation, bottling up his feelings and taking some very risky actions as a result. Ted trails along behind Nory on these adventures, determined to calm him. In taking on this new role, not only does Ted mature, but the "Solomon System" evolves into a new, even more solid, relationship. As Berge, writing in *School Library Journal* notes, "[t]he selfishness and immaturity of the parents is well balanced against the finely drawn personalities of the two brothers."[8] Adolescents will come to realize, with Ted, that some change in life is inevitable, but that true love and friendship allow for such change and provide a safety net for each individual. As in the York books, both the ease of the dialogue and its accurate reflection of the characters' feelings enable readers to empathize with the characters and to come away with a sense of comfort in the face of change.

The Keeper—Facing the Future
in the Absence of a Parent

In *The Keeper* (1986) Naylor turns once again to the metaphor of disease in exploring the issue of uncertainty. Unlike Dan, who still does not know at the end of the York series whether his father carries the Huntington's gene, Nick Karpinsky has had to face the reality that his father is mentally ill. Like Dan, Nick wonders about not only his father's future but about his own. "Is it inherited?" he blurts out when he finally has a chance to talk to a doctor (*The Keeper*, 208). Dr. Rothman is reassuring, explaining that medical experts are learning more all the time about the nature of schizophrenia and that its onset seems to have to do with body chemistry, something that is, in part, genetically determined. However, Rothman goes on to point out that Nick has shown

> a remarkable degree of mental health. . . the persuasive way you argued for your dad's admission. You faced up to the problem, you didn't just go under. It's time to get on with your own lives now. (*The Keeper*, 209)

Nick's struggles then are very similar to those of Ted and Dan. They all face family lives that are falling apart. Jacob Karpinsky's disintegration—and thus the disintegration of Nick's world—is made all the more frightening because Naylor is able to depict clearly the normalcy of Nick's world prior to this point. Until Jacob buys a gun and drives the family aimlessly around the city for hours stalking the "Communists" who are "after him," Nick's most pressing problems included his homework, his attempts to juggle a work schedule with other responsibilities, and his desire to go out with a girl living in the same apartment complex.

Long before the episode with the gun, Nick realizes that his father cannot acknowledge his illness, whereas his mother refuses to face the facts. Thus, early in the book, Nick tries to force the issue in order to get help for his father and relieve the incredible pressure under which they have been living. Initially, his efforts prove fruitless. He talks to the family priest. He talks to his uncle. His father presents himself to outsiders very rationally, so Nick's stories do not seem credible. Even while running up against brick walls in the quest for treatment for his dad, Nick intuitively understands that he has to take care of himself. He forms a circle of friends and eventually recognizes that true friendship will allow him the space he needs to talk about the situation. He seeks out the school nurse, asking advice, ostensibly for a "friend," about how to cope. In the end, it is the fact that the nurse, Miss Etting, has known about Jacob's history that provides Nick and his mother with the authority to commit Jacob to residential care without his personal consent.

But Nick is surprised to recognize guilt mingling with relief after his father is led away to a hospital ward. His father looks back at him, and Nick knows Jacob is very, very angry. Again Miss Etting intervenes. She reminds Nick

> Sometimes you have to decide which of two unhappy possibilities will be best. Those are the hard choices, Nick, but you did it. (*The Keeper*, 190)

Nick sleeps his first undisturbed sleep in months, sloughing off the worry of wondering what his dad was doing: roaming the apartment, hiding knives, creating towers of books to block the doors. Unfortunately, his exhaustion is so great that he does not awaken until his boss calls him at 3:45 the next afternoon, wondering where he is. When Nick gets to the store, he takes the next step in dealing with his family situation. For the first time, he admits publicly that his father is mentally ill. Admitting this to others also means that Nick and his mother have to acknowledge the uncertainties that will always confront them. Nobody can predict whether Jacob's condition will improve with time and treatment. Also, they will never be certain how others will react to the disclosure of Jacob's condition. Lois, Nick's date for the big spring dance—his first-ever date—backs out at the last minute. The dialogue between Lois and Nick as she breaks the date, with all its underlying implications, rings true. Anyone who has ever been "dumped" by someone unwilling to explain, unable even to see the limitations of stereotypic thinking, can relate to Nick's heartache:

> "Have you heard anymore about your dad? I mean, will he recover?"
> "We don't know yet," Nick told her.
> There was an awkward pause, and then Lois spoke with a rush: "Look, Nick, I really hope you won't take this the wrong way, but I was thinking—with your father sick and everything—maybe you really don't feel like going to the dance. . . . I mean, you must be worried to death, and I . . . well, if I was in your place, I don't think I'd feel like going *anywhere*, but I just wanted to say if you didn't feel like going, it's really all right. I mean, you know Chuck Peters—from Biology? Well, he asked me after you did, and he still doesn't have a date, and I just thought maybe . . ."
> . . . The message came through loud and clear. It was probably all over school by now. Nick Karpinsky's dad was a psycho. Lois didn't want to be seen with him. (*The Keeper*, 198–99)

But Nick also discovers that his real friends stick by him, support him, and even increase their respect for him once they realize how strong he has been. Naylor ends the novel with a poignant scene in which Nick cries, forcing out the tears "until there were none left" (*The Keeper*, 211), after acknowledging that he is just going to have to live with the ups and downs:

> [T]here was nothing Nick could do to change matters. It was time to concentrate on things he could do something about—his own life. (*The Keeper*, 212)

And he does. He washes his face, tells his mother he is going out, knocks on the door of a neighboring apartment, and spontaneously asks Karen for a date. The reader knows, as the two young people walk out into the rain that is washing the air clean, that Nick will not only endure whatever the future has in store but will find his own way through it with dignity and hope. Naylor's well-developed character—a young man who is both insightful and scared, strong but needy, in some ways mature beyond his years but in others unsophisticated—provides a model for adolescents trying to clear a path into the future through all the chaos of the present.

A review in *Booklist* describes *The Keeper* as "a sensitively wrought novel with no happy ending but certainly with an affirmation of individual strength and emotional survival in the face of adversity."[9] This analysis reinforces Naylor's own perception of the book as one designed to provide hope to young readers facing difficult, uncertain times. *The Keeper* has also been praised for its discerning characterization, its adeptness in describing the gradual disintegration of a family's comfort and happiness, and its intelligent treatment of the subject of mental illness.[10]

Naylor was able to depict so accurately both Jacob's deterioration and Nick's responses to his family situation in part because of her skill as a writer and in part because she had experienced Nick's circumstances herself. She loosely based his story on her adult book *Crazy Love: An Autobiographical Account of Marriage and Madness* (1977; hereafter cited as *Crazy Love*), in which she describes with both humor and poignancy her own education as a result of her first husband's mental illness. Many incidents found in *The Keeper* originated from Naylor's own history. Nick's growth toward acceptance of the situation and assumption of responsibility for his own life mirror Naylor's own development from sheltered adolescent female into a more mature and independent woman.

Jacob yells at his wife and Nick, undermining their confidence just as Naylor's first husband belittled her, calling her shallow, self-conscious, semiliterate, and abominably ignorant. She says that she began her married life with little self-confidence and after two years had even less. But she had an inner strength that she later confers on Nick. Even while her husband challenged her every idea and decision, she nevertheless made friends of her own, auditioned for and became a member of the university choir, and continued writing with success. In *The Keeper*, one of the first signs that Jacob is losing touch with reality is that he begins to change jobs with increasing frequency. Naylor can portray with accuracy Nick's unease because she lived through several years during which her first husband could not commit to any one job.

When Nick cannot convince his mother to seek medical help for Jacob, and when he therefore feels trapped in a surreal world dominated by a father who acts erratically, he relies on the routines of school and work to keep him sane. Naylor describes how she herself found security in habit and "repetition of mundane tasks." She grew fond of making the bed and reading the mail because they were routine events in an otherwise chaotic life (*Crazy Love*, 94).

Firsthand knowledge of the importance of having an outlet during a crisis enables Naylor to describe clearly Nick's need for a caring listener. Although her own family was not particularly given to physical demonstrations of affection, Naylor recalls the importance of knowing that they cared about her and wanted to hear about the truth of her situation. One Christmas she called to tell her parents that her husband's illness would prevent them from returning home for the holidays. She broke down, letting her grief erupt, and realized how long it had been since she had experienced a normal response from someone sane. Her mother did not try to offer solutions; she did not offer to help. She merely said, with genuine affection and concern, "Phyllis, I'm so sorry." Naylor remembers that this response—just a "sharing of feeling"—was what she needed in order to garner the strength to carry on (*Crazy Love*, 96).

Neither Nick nor his mother feel confident that they have done the right thing in committing Jacob against his will. Nick's fear that he is somehow responsible for his father's situation echoes Naylor's own self-doubt and confusion about whether she was at all accountable for her husband's condition. In *Crazy Love* she writes

> Was it worth it to drag a patient kicking and screaming for treatment? How could a patient get well knowing that every breath he took cost more than his family could afford? How long before my own resentment grew so strong I could not hide it? ... What about the feeling that I had driven one man mad and nobody else would want me? If we separated, if I washed my hands of him finally and just gave up—would I go on worrying about him the rest of my natural life anyway? (*Crazy Love*, 150)

Just as Nick has a Miss Etting, a health care professional, to listen to him and help him recognize the limits of his responsibility for his father, Naylor had a social worker who helped her explore these issues and come to the conclusion that she should seek divorce. Like Nick, having made the decision to get on with her own life, she felt drained. She slept deeply for the first time in years knowing she did not have to worry about whether her husband was going to find the steak knives and harm himself or others with them.

However, Naylor's ordeal was in some ways even more difficult than Nick's. Jacob's admission into the hospital, once Miss Etting arrives on the scene, is relatively easy to accomplish. Nick still has his mother to turn to for support; he still has the structure of school to provide a sense of security. Naylor found that making the decision to seek divorce was much easier than actually getting one. At the time—the late 1950s—seeking divorce on the grounds of mental illness required that the psychotic spouse be declared insane, that this diagnosis be carried over a set number of consecutive years, usually five, that the spouse be confined, and that at least three doctors had to concur that the individual was incurable. Few doctors are willing to state in writing that a patient will never get well. In addition, her husband's parents had become his guardians; they did not believe in divorce and so were unwilling to allow Naylor to pursue legal separation. Eventually, Naylor had to have three doctors declare that *she* was ill, certifying that *she* would need extensive therapy and care as a result of the stress and strain of living with her husband. Because existing law mandated that a husband—and his guardians—were responsible for all the spouse's medical debts—thus requiring her in-laws to pay for her therapy if there was no divorce—Naylor finally persuaded her husband's parents to sign the divorce papers on his behalf.

Nevertheless, Naylor usually finds a way to interject a note of humor no matter how serious the issues underlying a novel. Her faculty for using contrast to lighten the tone is evident in *Crazy Love*. She writes that she and her first husband were the antithesis of each other: He is compulsive and she is "compulsively careless." She also writes with understated precision, creating a humorous, lighter touch, while making more serious points.

Furthermore, Naylor's own skill in focusing on the tiny details that make life worth living, a skill developed as another coping mechanism, is one she gives many of her characters, including Nick. She describes how she read newspapers ravenously, with a wonderful appetite for information about people and events from all over the world, about earthquakes, famine, war, and trouble of any sort. She learned to appreciate tiny pleasures, like the warmth of the bed, the taste of an apple, the coolness of a drink of water. Similarly, Nick seeks refuge in his job at Mr. Perona's deli. One afternoon, for instance, a shipment of cheese arrives, and Nick revels in the work involved in cutting it into chunks, wrapping it, weighing it, labeling it, and stacking it in the refrigerator. Throwing himself into the work of dusting shelves, sweeping the floor, hauling barrels of food to new locations, he enjoys the way his body reacts to this physical labor, and he responds to the rhythms involved in just moving from moment to moment, getting the job done.

An ability to give the reader a sense of the physical environment and of the character's place within it is a strength of Naylor's craft. Her skill in this area grew in part out of her life experiences in coping with her first husband's problems, as did her concern that adolescents need to find ways to cope with the grave uncertainties of life.

4. Becoming an Individual within the Family Context: *To Shake a Shadow, A String of Chances, The Year of the Gopher, Send No Blessings,* and *Ice*

Dan, Ted and Nory, and Nick—as Naylor herself had to do—move into more mature understandings of the world and their relationship to it because of the uncertain family situations with which they have to cope. The characters in *To Shake a Shadow, A String of Chances, The Year of the Gopher, Send No Blessings,* and *Ice* confront a somewhat different set of dilemmas. Each of the young people in these books struggles to determine a sense of self that ultimately must *transcend* a definition of self based on their positions within their families.

The main characters in these novels wrestle with the question "Who am I?" and discover that they cannot rely on past history to provide them with an answer. They must make some decisions about their values, their goals, their beliefs, and their futures in order to come to terms with themselves—and they then have to deal with their families in new ways as a result.

To Shake a Shadow and *Ice*—Casting Off the Dark Clouds of Family Association

At the end of *The Keeper*, Nick walks out into a world washed clean and fresh by rain, reflecting the sense of newness and optimism he feels about his personal life. Naylor opens *To Shake a Shadow* (1967; hereafter cited as *Shake*) with a description of an autumn landscape full of color and promise, a description mirroring the feeling of excitement Brad Willson has about his upcoming school year. Soon, however, the weather changes. An unseasonal heat wave makes the air heavy and oppressive, reflecting the tension Brad comes to recognize as undermining the routine equilibrium of Willson family life. At school, the "Skids," a group of racially prejudiced bullies, have begun to intensify their activity level, and the bulk of the student body will not open their mouths for fear of reprisal, creating a sense of unease for Brad there as well as at home.

When the weather breaks and the leaves abandon the trees, leaving them bare and littering the sidewalks, things come to a head in Brad's life. He arrives at school on a morning he thinks is like any other, only to find himself the object of pitying stares and uneasy looks. The story of his father's income tax evasion has been in the morning paper, and Brad's friends have learned more about Brad's family life than he has known himself.

Having the black and white outlook on right and wrong so common among adolescents, Brad feels totally betrayed—not only by his father, whom he has revered, but also by his mother, who has known the truth for some time but has hidden it from the children. Brad screams at his mother when she tries to talk to him about the situation.

> "You *don't* know how I feel! . . . All these weeks—I've known something was wrong, but no one would tell me. Talk about Dad being dishonest! You're so blind you can't even see it honestly yourself. All those stupid excuses you've thought up—'not like stealing from a person'—'everybody does it.' He's a *criminal*, Mom, a common, ordinary criminal, and all the blubbering in the world isn't going to make him anything else. . . ."

Brad moved away from her and sat down at his desk, his
head in his hands and his heart in his mouth. There was no love
in him for anybody, including himself. (*Shake*, 34–35)

Brad's quest throughout the rest of the novel is one for both a
new relationship with his father and for a new sense of self, for a
self he can once again value and respect in spite of his family's
dishonor. Feeling repulsed and betrayed, filled with self loathing,
Brad has a difficult time moving forward with his life. He bedevils
his mother and father by refusing to eat at the family table, refusing to interact in any way. When his sister becomes the object of
stereotypical thinking, his rage intensifies: At school, another
child's money is missing, and the teacher forces Judith—perceived as the possible culprit because she is the child of a thief—to
take off her shoes and socks in front of the whole class in order to
determine whether she has taken the money and hidden it. Brad
decides that if the world refuses to trust Judith and him because
their father has made a mistake, then "if you were going to be
punished anyway, then do something worth punishing" (*Shake*,
54–55). This hostility induces him to vandalize the school, steal-
ing a tape recorder for which he has no need except as a symbol of
his rebellion and anger.

Fortunately, Brad, an inexperienced thief, is caught. He is
required to spend time with Mr. Corday, the school guidance
counselor and the father of one of his friends. Again Naylor shows
the importance of finding someone who will listen without judg-
ing; Brad begins to look forward to his visits to Corday's office
because there he can express himself honestly. Through these
conversations he starts to recognize the limitations that have
always existed in his home situation. Another source of support is
Lenny, the son of Russian immigrants, a boy from a social stra-
tum very different from Brad's own. Brad turns to Lenny because
he no longer feels comfortable around his previous friends, whose
relationships with him have been based on a shared sense of place
within the town's hierarchy. Naylor counterbalances descriptions
of the Willson home, which, on the surface, has always appeared
to be a rather ideal environment rich in the traditions of inher-

ited wealth, with Lenny's. At Lenny's house, family members make it a point to know each other well and find much to genuinely like about each other. Lenny and his parents argue, play games, joke, share good times and bad in a much more open and giving way than Brad's family does, and Brad is surprised to discover he envies Lenny.

At first Brad blames his parents for everything with which he finds fault in his life. He even tries to say that it is his dad's fault he stole the recorder. With wonderfully convoluted logic, he argues that had his dad not stolen money, Judith would not have been embarrassed in front of her peers, and then he would not have gotten angry enough to steal the recorder. With Mr. Corday's help, Brad comes to realize *he* made the decision to take the recorder—and that *he* will have to make decisions about how he wants to live the rest of his life.

Brad also learns to recognize the nature of human fallibility, something that characters in many other Naylor titles do. Part of growing up in Naylor's world is understanding that there is good and bad in everyone, and, as a result, individuals have to give voice to the good within themselves. Brad discovers, for instance, that when he presents himself as an object of pity, his friends treat him in the pitying manner he so dislikes; conversely, when he reaches out to them in friendship, rather than withdrawing into himself or lashing out moodily, they respond in kind (*Shake*, 86).

Now that his father is under such a cloud, Brad determines that he misses what he "*thought* he [his dad] used to be" and therefore wonders if he is missing an imaginary person. Mr. Corday speaks for Naylor here:

> It's true that your dad isn't all you thought he was, and that's a fact we just have to accept . . . but he still exists, for whatever he is, and there's good in him along with the bad. That's true of all of us—you, me—nobody's one or the other. But sometimes it hurts to find that out. (*Shake*, 78)

Feeling intense guilt at having stolen his brother Wally's car, Brad analyzes both his father's behavior and his own responses to the situation. It gradually dawns on him that he cannot forgive his father until he forgives himself for not being perfect.

Lenny teaches Brad a lot about the nature of forgiveness and friendship. This novel was published in 1967, a time when an individual's class, religious affiliation, ethnicity, and race often were determiners of his or her place within the societal structure. Naylor presents an alternative to such thinking. Lenny is Jewish. Speaking with an elitist view of her place within the town's social fabric that her husband's actions have yet to upset, Brad's mother wonders if her son's wild behavior has been caused by his association with the other boy. She notes that Lenny "comes from a different kind of home than ours—financially and educationally and. . . ."

> "Morally?" Brad said cuttingly, and his mother blushed.
> "I'm not questioning his character," she said hastily, "but—well—they are Jewish, you know." (*Shake*, 112)

Hearing his mother voice these words awakens Brad to the realization that Lenny and his family have lived their entire lives with many strikes against them, given the nature of the town's social structure. And yet Lenny has not viewed his religion, his family's economic status, or his parents' lack of proficiency in English as disadvantages. Lenny has always acted with genuine friendship and concern, has accepted Brad's moodiness, and has tried to offer advice even when Brad could not accept it. Brad knows he has to be the person—the good person—Lenny has always seen him to be, and he makes a difficult decision to stand up for his friend, to forgive himself for his past behavior, and to move forward with his life.

Brad decides to tackle the Skids, who are planning to attack Lenny just because he is different, in their eyes, and they are expecting Brad's help. After ruining Wally's car, Brad's self-respect sinks so low that he turns away even from Lenny. In doing so he opens himself to the Skids, who play on the desires of those students who crave belonging and who feel good about themselves only when they put others down. His initiation involves luring Lenny into a good location for a beating. But he comes to his senses at the last minute, realizing he is sinking to a level of behavior that does not reflect his true values. He organizes a group of his older friends to help him take on the Skids, warns Lenny about the impending action, and in a physical battle that symbolizes the emotional struggles raging in his head, he fights the Skids and the demons warring for control of his mind and heart.

As the novel ends, Naylor introduces another key theme that runs throughout her writing: Hard work for honest ends is a terrific antidote for anger, self-pity, self-hatred, and the hatred of others. Brad gets a job as a stock boy in a clothing store. As was true of Nick in *The Keeper*, the intense physical activity, the structure of the tasks, and the companionship involved in getting the work done make him feel good, and that good feeling helps him rebuild his sense of self-esteem. The reader is left with the impression that no matter what happens to Mr. Willson, Brad will not only be able to make good choices about his own life, but will eventually even come to like his father and care about him in a more realistic way than he did as the story began.

Thirteen-year-old Chrissa, from the 1995 book *Ice*, is, in some ways, the female counterpart to Brad. Her father, Nick, has been missing from her life for three years, and in her darkest moments, she blames herself for this absence. Perhaps if she had shared his sense of adventure, been willing to take risks, been "the kind of daughter a dad would want to be around" (*Ice*, 17), he would not have disappeared. But when she is forced to spend a year with Nick's mother in the country, she begins to suspect that Nick has a darker secret that is responsible for his departure from her life.

Gram and Chrissa struggle to develop a relationship, but Chrissa feels frozen inside herself, desperate to learn the truth about her father, lonely in a new school, and afraid at first of the country sounds so different from New York City noises. But when two evangelists appear on the scene and try to dupe Gram into turning over her valuable property rights to their "church," Chrissa decides to take action. She spends a good deal of time looking for her father and, at the same time, for proof that Sister Harmony and her nephew are frauds. In the meantime, she takes on a baby-sitting job, and her success in caring for two young children is a boost to her self-esteem. As other Naylor protagonists do, Chrissa learns the value of work in other ways. She does half the housework and half the cooking, helps the neighbors pick apples during fall harvest, and thus comes to appreciate the good feelings engendered by accomplishing tasks and contributing to the larger order.

But Chrissa is convinced that she will not be able to know and accept herself until she knows the truth about her father. It turns out that, like Brad's father, Nick is a criminal. He is incarcerated in Watertown Prison, which is why he has not been to see her for so long. When her grandmother finally reveals the truth and confirms what she has been piecing together, Chrissa is relieved. Her grandmother has been reluctant to tell her the story because, as she says, "Sometimes I look at you, honey, at all your hurts, and see a girl waiting for something to come along and change things—like a bush waiting for spring. Sometimes we have to *be* spring, Chrissa; *we* have to be the ones that do the changing" (*Ice*, 171). Chrissa agrees, points out that they are doing a lot of changing, and they hug, united in their willingness to work together to move forward with their lives.

Chrissa is also helped in this effort when she discovers that Thad Hewlitt, a neighbor boy with whom she is developing a tentative relationship, has known about her father all along and has liked her anyway. She begins to understand that she cannot let her father and his actions rule her life. She has to take responsibility for being the kind of person she wants to be. When the estranged father of her two baby-sitting charges attempts to kidnap them during a massive ice storm, she saves their lives. Reflecting on her good deed, Chrissa perceives that she is well on her way to becoming "her own kind of person" (*Ice*, 198). As Casey, writing in a starred review of *Ice* in *School Library Journal*, says, "Empowered by her own sense of fitness, she faces her demons, the parents who have failed her, and forgives."[1]

A String of Chances—Developing a
Personal Set of Religious Values

Evie Hutchins, in *A String of Chances* (1982; hereafter cited as *String*), like Brad and Chrissa, must figure out who she is, must come to accept her strengths and limitations, and then must begin the process of accepting her family and all their idiosyncratic ways. The Hutchins family is more than a bit unusual, although having grown up in its bosom, Evie does not realize how different her life has been from that of most of her peers. Mr. Hutchins is a self-educated preacher for a small, conservative congregation with fundamentalist beliefs. Mrs. Hutchins spends her days catering to the needs of an assortment of adults who live in Evie's house under arrangements similar to those made for foster children. On Sundays, the whole clan gathers around the dinner table, and their conversations are predictably the same. No questions are asked; no real discussion takes place, except about topics such as the food on the table.

However, 16-year-old Evie is filled with uncertainty. For several years she has kept a journal in which she has recorded favorite quotes from authors whose ideas have started an itch in her to explore the basis of her parents' faith. Emerson, Melville, Chief Crawfoot, and Milton have begun to broaden her horizons at the time this novel opens. Thus, when the opportunity presents itself for Evie to live apart from her family for a time, she leaps at it. Her cousin, Donna, is about to deliver her first child. Evie moves across town to live with Donna in order to help make the house into a home and to help care for the baby once it arrives.

While with Donna and her husband Tom, the artistic part of Evie's character begins to bloom. She realizes she responds to colors, beautiful music, aesthetically pleasing objects:

> To begin with scarcely nothing at all—a lump of clay, a piece of wood, a basket of sewing scraps, a sheet of paper—and create, in turn, a bowl, a carving, a quilt, or a poem—that was what she wanted to do. (*String*, 26)

Donna and Evie decide to open their own shop, a place to sell their own handicrafts. Evie is delighted with this articulation of a long-held dream. Now,

> for the first time Evie had begun to see how all the unsorted threads of her interests might be woven into a single cloth, had felt she had a grip on her life, a direction. She wouldn't just wind up clerking at the five and ten. (*String*, 28)

Evie's desire to be a "maker" is not unique in Naylor's world. In Naylor's books, the desire to create is celebrated, and characters who long to express themselves through acts of creation—Evie and Donna Jean, Jed from *Wrestle the Mountain*, the photographer who is the main character in *The Dark of the Tunnel*, among others—are supported in their quest by the author, who is herself an originator. Reminded during an interview about the number of her characters who do things with their hands, she says,

> That was me, and that *is* me. I would rather sing than go to a concert. I would rather paint than go to an art gallery. I want to be in there, doing. It is important to me, being in on the ground floor, and not just being an observer.

But Evie's parents do not fully understand this drive to create. Nor do they appreciate her growing need to question their religious teachings, to articulate a basis of faith for herself.

Three events conspire to force Evie into this questioning stance. First of all, when Evie leaves for Donna Jean's, Evie's family takes in Matt Jewel, who needs a steadying influence and a job for the summer. Matt has a somewhat shady reputation. He is known as being rather wild, and he has always pulled at Evie's loyalties. Matt shakes up Sunday dinner by actually asking questions about the sermon Evie's father had delivered. He genuinely wants to know how those gathered around the table can distinguish feeling great because of the presence of God from feeling exhilarated because they have been successful climbing a mountain or reaching a state of transcendence during meditation. Evie's dad not only accepts Matt's questions and deals with them seriously, but he also tells others at the table, who have treated Matt with condescension, that nobody in his house will look down on anyone who is seriously engaged in a spiritual quest. Mr. Hutchins tells Evie emphatically that everyone in the room, sitting around the table, is on a spiritual journey, and that no individual, including himself, ever goes as far as he or she can (*String*, 182).

Rather than being excited to have Matt stirring things up at home, Evie is angry. Matt has just blurted out all those questions she has buried inside herself for so long. "Matt waded in right where angels feared to tread, and Father treated him like a little lost lamb" (*String*, 184). But Evie knows her anger is partly directed at herself. When Matt points out that there is always only "one idea going around the table and it's served up as the main course" (*String*, 187) every day, Evie has to acknowledge the truth of his observation, and she begins to reflect in new ways on the habits and patterns of interaction to which she has become accustomed.

Second, Evie meets Chris, a gifted drummer who has come to town to spend the summer working in the general store. As in the "Alice" books, Naylor's descriptions of the deliciousness of first love capture that experience with exquisite precision:

> They walked slowly, making it last. . . . They stopped, once, halfway to the road, to listen to a mockingbird going through its repertoire. Every so often it would throw in the plaintive cry of a catbird, and then they would laugh. The whole earth seemed drenched in the fragrance of honeysuckle. . . .
> It was not any one thing that exhilarated her—not the touch of his hand against hers, or the caress of his thumb, or the way his arm encircled her waist there, at last, in the pine-scented darkness. Not even the way his lips had grazed her forehead when he said good night at the pond. It was the easy way it all happened, one thing gliding into the next. (*String*, 117–18)

Evie, an artist, is attracted to Chris, the musician, for a number of reasons, including his gift for drumming. As they try to determine where their relationship might lead, Evie recognizes that Chris's presence in her life, like Matt's, has caused her to question her parents' beliefs. For instance, she spends an afternoon in Chris's room listening with wonder to him play. She knows, as she does so, that she is violating her parents' code of behavior, but she cannot see the problem. She wonders, "How do you grow up without growing away? And if that's not possible, how do you grow away without tearing everyone apart?" (*String*, 152).

The third and most important element of Evie's disquiet is her struggle to come to terms with the death of Donna and Tom's baby, a result of SIDS, "sudden infant death syndrome." Evie has been almost as much a part of Josh's life as have his parents. When Tom returns to work and Donna begins taking naps in the afternoon, Evie is the one who walks the floor with Joshua while her cousin sleeps. Evie soothes his colicky spells. It is "Evie who nuzzled his tiny rosebud ear and drank in his sweet baby scent" (*String*, 82).

In Donna and Tom's house, filled with the scents and sounds of Joshua, a product of his parents' love, Naylor creates an idyllic world, one that Evie sees in sharp contrast to her own home. Donna and Tom talk to each other, feel free to disagree, share responsibilities, and work together to create a shared sense of future in which each will support the other's continued development. But Joshua dies, and Donna and Tom's relationship is put to the test. Evie is heartbroken, and all her questions of faith, questions about the very existence of God come pouring forth. She confronts her father, begging him to help Joshua's death make some sort of sense from a theological standpoint. Her father very calmly explains his position: God did not intend for Joshua to die, but after the fact, will find a way to use the situation to "glorify" creation.

Rejecting his explanation, Evie lashes out at her father, accusing him of spouting words with no substance behind them. Knowing that not only has she hurt her father but also that she meant to do so, Evie is not sure whether she is so angry on Joshua's behalf or on her own. She is certain, however, that voicing her anger so clearly is an act that separates her from the accepting child she had once been. And, in finally acknowledging her need to question, to craft an identity, including a set of religious beliefs of her own, she begins to find her way into a real relationship with God. Evie realizes she had been asking her father to prove God's existence for her because "I wanted an object for my anger, something that I could touch, a God that I could accuse and condemn. And yet, in spite of everything, something is here. I can't hold it in my hand, but I can sense it" (*String*, 224–25).

Later Naylor tells the reader that Evie feels that this presence is both "beyond herself and in herself. There was no name for it exactly, but for want of something better, she called it God. Whether it could be reconciled with her father's God she didn't yet know" (*String*, 225). Mr. Hutchins is, like Alice's father, able to accept his daughter's need to struggle with difficult questions by herself. Also like Alice's father, he reassures his daughter that he will always love and support her as she matures into selfhood. Mr. Hutchins states, "The important thing is we're in this life together, and we shouldn't forget that" (*String*, 235). As Roger Sutton, in a review for *School Library Journal*, noted, Naylor's ability to create a realistic story about a young woman's movement toward independence using a style that is "sensible and warm, but not florid"[2] is one of the reasons the novel has achieved such critical success.

Evie's spiritual quest reflects Naylor's own as a young woman. Like Evie's, Naylor notes that her own doubts began in her childhood but that she did not verbalize them because her family's life revolved around church. Her mother taught Sunday school; her father was Sunday school superintendent and lay leader. Naylor's Maryland grandparents took in wards of the state, so that during her summer visits to Marbury, Naylor encountered the real-life equivalents of Evie's Sister Ozzie and the aphasic Mr. Schmidt, and she attended her grandfather's church, where he preached a religious vision similar to that of Mr. Hutchins.

Naylor's parents read from a large Bible storybook each night, and she remembers being able to put herself into those stories: "I was a fellow traveler with the Israelites on their journey to the promised land. I would never, I was sure, have worshipped the Golden Calf or mocked Elisha."[3] But even as a child, she wondered about the "whys" of such stories in ways she knew her parents would not understand. For instance, she was taught that the Israelites had to march around Jericho seven times to make its walls come tumbling down because "it stood in the way" of their progress to the Promised Land. But if the Israelites could march around Jericho, wondered Naylor, how could Jericho have stood in the way? She recounts wondering, too, why God struck dead one of the men charged with carrying the Ark of the Covenant just because he reached out his hand to steady it at a point when it began to tip. Being certain she would have reacted in just this way to save a precious object, she questioned, "Didn't anybody get points for using his head?"[4]

At the end of *A String of Chances*, Evie is able to define God and her belief structure only in very nebulous terms, a reflection of Naylor's own religious framework. Mr. Hutchins appears more accepting of Evie's position than Naylor's own parents, whom she describes as being made "uneasy, upset, worried" by her questioning. She says, again using terms similar to those she allows Evie to use,

> The only truthful answer possible, it seems to me, is that I am too small, and the universe too big, ever to understand it all. I am as uncomfortable with people who insist that their talents are gifts from God as I am with those who claim that accidents and illness are punishments from the Almighty. They do seem related, for if God has chosen to favor some, then He has apparently decided to short-change others. And because I cannot believe that a loving God would do this, I continue to read, and think and wonder.[5]

Naylor says that, although she was able to discuss her position on issues such as whether only Christians could be "saved," she feels her mother never really accepted her arguments. For her mother, the bottom line was that those who do not believe in her particular Christian faith—one that includes heaven and hell—will not, at the time of the Last Judgment, find themselves in heaven. And Naylor is sad to recall the grief her mother must have felt in believing that she would therefore not be reunited with either Naylor or Naylor's brother in the afterlife.[6] Having experienced the pain of the seeker whose quest pulls him or her away from the family belief structure, Naylor clearly conveys Evie's anguish in hurting her father in *String of Chances*. The novel won a place in the "Notable Children's Trade Books in Social Studies" in *Social Education* for the clarity and realism of the depiction of a religious quest within a finely drawn small town setting.[7]

The Year of the Gopher— Finding a Career Path for Oneself

In *The Year of the Gopher* (1987; hereafter cited as *Gopher*) Naylor's protagonist, George, does not engage in the kind of spiritual quest that pulls Evie Hutchins away from her family. Like Evie and Naylor herself, George does sometimes wonder about theological questions, such as why "acts of God" are almost always horrible events—floods and hurricanes—and why a particular individual is hit by lightning. But George's main problem is his fight for the right to make his own decisions—in the here and now—about his future.

The second of four children and the oldest boy, George is expected to follow in his father's footsteps and become a lawyer from an Ivy League school. And he is expected to live up to the reputation for scholastic excellence established by his older sister, Trish. But during his senior year of high school, George begins to question his parents' vision of his future. He no longer finds it amusing when his father strategically places a newspaper article—where George is sure to see it—about the income levels of various professions. When Mr. Richards arranges a week off from work in order to fly from Minnesota to visit colleges with George on the East Coast—a trip George has no interest in taking—George knows he must find a way to be heard.

The experience is a disaster. George knows his dad cares about him, and he is grateful for that concern, but he thinks,

> I regret that I have but one life to give for my father. . . . I felt
> miserable, but something told me that if I didn't stand up to
> him now, I'd be lost. If I let him put me on the old railroad, I'd
> never get off, and before you knew it, Jess and Ollie would be on
> it, too. Somebody had to look out for them, especially for Ollie.
> (*Gopher*, 42–43)

Ollie is the youngest member of the Richards family is, in
George's words, "different." Ollie just cannot grasp academic
material quickly, and he is slow to understand new concepts. Mr.
and Mrs. Richards find this aspect of Ollie hard to accept, and
when his first report card from seventh grade contains all Cs and
a D in Spanish, they wonder what the next disappointment from
him will be. George is incensed to learn that his parents do not
think Ollie cares about disappointing them.

George is further upset to hear his father say that *George* goes
through life without a care in the world. George himself feels he
has been worried since age four. He recalls being worried in nurs-
ery school that nobody would pick him up. He recalls that he
began worrying about marriage as early as kindergarten, and that
by age seven, he was compulsive about his worries.

Thus George begins to realize that his parents have very little
knowledge of who their children are and who they want to be.
When Ollie, crying over a Spanish assignment, hints that he
might drop Spanish the next semester, Mrs. Richards says he
should not be ridiculous. She admonishes him, saying he cannot
go through life giving up when something becomes difficult. She
cites numerous examples of times when Ollie has abandoned an
activity: clarinet lessons, the science fair, the merit badge in
astronomy. George, however, notes that all these projects were
chosen by his parents, not by Ollie. He goes on to reflect on Ollie's
experiences with Boy Scouts, an organization Ollie had wanted to
join because of his love for camping.

> Two weeks after he'd signed up, Dad started him working on a
> merit badge—had his Scouting career all laid out before him:
> Tenderfoot as soon as he could make it, Second Class by age

thirteen, First Class by fourteen, then Star, Life, and Eagle. You couldn't just be a Scout in our family; you had to be the best there was. (*Gopher*, 59)

Later, George determines that his parents *need* "successful" children, children who can make them proud, because such children come from successful parents. His mother and dad, he starts to understand, define themselves and measure their success as parents by their children's accomplishments. He also realizes that his parents are the victims of similar expectations—that their parents had operated in the same way. George then makes a conscious decision: He will break the chain. He sabotages all of his college applications, and the rejections begin to arrive.

Mrs. Richards figures out what George has done and confronts him, asking why he did not tell her and her husband that he did not want to go to college. George replies,

"I said it every way I knew how, but you weren't listening. . . . You don't care about me, you don't care about my education, you only care how it makes you *look*. . . . Somebody had to make the break. I'm not going to end up at an Ivy League school with a bottle of Maalox just to please you and Dad." (*Gopher*, 75–76)

Naylor juxtaposes Mr. and Mrs. Richards' expectations for their children with the hopes held by another mother, Shirl, for her daughter Heather. Shirl is a clerk at the garden center where George works after high school graduation. Every day she checks in with Heather to ask how many hearts the girl has broken that day. Shirl's desires that her daughter be popular, pretty, the object of every boy's unrequited love, although quite different from those of George's parents, are equally destructive. George's heart goes out to Heather. He recognizes that it is the *girl's* heart that is breaking—not only because she does not receive the attention from boys her mother thinks she deserves, but also because her mother cannot seem to value her as an individual. His experiences in observing Shirl and Heather not only affirm his decision to make a dramatic break with his parents, but they also lead him eventually to decide to become a school guidance counselor.

Naylor's skill as a developer of character allows the reader to believe George's slow transformation from a somewhat self-centered adolescent into a young man of substance, a person who has begun to determine some core beliefs around which to build his life. As George moves through "the year of the gopher"—his year after graduation spent running errands (being a "gofer"), doing manual labor and some sales clerking at a garden center, and then riding a bike to deliver packages and messages around the city—in small increments, he increasingly takes charge of finding his own way through life. His announcement of his possible career choice and of his decision to enroll at the local university ring true because, as Steve Matthews writes in *School Library Journal*, Naylor "stops short of patness and reaffirms the complexity and pain of coming of age."[8]

While portraying George as a young man driven by hormones and concerned about his looks, his affiliations with his friends, and his need to rebel against the family structure, Naylor also shows George, through action and dialogue, as a caring, thoughtful person who genuinely wants to help others. For example, he acts responsibly when he is the designated driver for the evening, refusing alcohol and trying to keep his friends in line when they have had too much to drink. George recognizes the difficulties his younger sister, Jeri, is having with an older boyfriend who is somewhat abusive. He talks to Jeri compassionately. With his friends, he takes action to ensure that she will not be bothered again. George also voluntarily spends time with his grandfather. Realizing that Shirl would like him to be more than a fellow employee and recognizing her efforts to pull him into her life as preliminary sexual advances, George also perceives that his manager will not take a stand on Shirl's behavior. As a result, he quits a job he enjoys rather than be led into a compromising relationship. Thus the reader develops an appreciation for his strengths that, ironically, his parents have yet to learn, causing plot tension that pulls the reader along through George's story.

The development of George's ability and willingness to construct his own value structure underlies the plot of the novel. Very early in the story, Naylor describes Karen, who is, from George's perspective, the most gorgeous girl in the school. A friend of George's, Jake, works at a local pharmacy and tells his gang of friends that he sold birth control pills to Karen. George can just imagine how Jake probably smirked and winked knowingly at the girl when handing her the prescription. George thinks,

> I would have picked up that sack without hardly looking at it, then rung up the price—sort of a reflex action, you know. I'd ask her something about school while I stapled the bag shut, and I imagined how she'd appreciate it. (*Gopher*, 11)

When George's social studies teacher remarks that to someone blind, the ugliest person in terms of outward appearance might seem the most beautiful, George earnestly ponders the idea. Later in the book, he and his friends sneak into an over-18 club, where they play "Selectrocution." At the end of the evening, those in the club who—via computer interactive technology—have not received any ballots positively describing their physical attributes are "selectrocuted." George thinks about the women who are not beauty queens, and he sends them anonymous messages, complimenting one on her hair, another on her legs; he even gets one of his companions to do the same.

Therefore, when George falls into a sexual relationship with Maureen, a girl in his class who has been actively pursuing him for several years, the reader believes him when he expresses discomfort with the situation. He takes Maureen to the prom and then follows her lead afterward, going along with her arrangements for a picnic in a cemetery and not protesting when she initiates a more intimate relationship. He says, "I just let it happen—just swam with the tide. . . . I didn't feel especially proud of myself" (*Gopher*, 89).

George is not above bragging to his friends about his new level of sexual experience, but as he becomes more able to express his own values and gains skill in acting upon them, he tells Maureen good-bye. He learns that *he* is responsible for his future—whether in school, a career, or a relationship. When George next asks a girl to spend time with him, he takes things more slowly, working on finding common ground, on becoming true companions.

Early in the book, Mrs. Richards tells her son to stay out of the home of Dave Hahn, a long-time friend of George's, when she discovers that Dave's father is bisexual. At first, George, somewhat uncomfortable with this information about Mr. Hahn, does stay away. But as he gets to know more about the man, he discovers Mr. Hahn just wants to be accepted as he is, for who he is. George can certainly identify with that desire. This empathy spurs George to action; by the end of the book, he is willing to go to Dave's house and play poker with father and son in spite of his parents' admonitions. Also, George begins to realize that his grandfather earnestly wishes to retain a sense of independence and autonomy. George stands up for his grandfather's right to live as he chooses, arguing forcefully against his parents and other relatives who want to direct the older man's life.

George's move toward selfhood causes turmoil in the Richards' home. After it is clear that George is not going to go to college, the atmosphere in the house freezes. One small step at a time, however, Naylor also shows George's parents changing. Mrs. Richards decides to refuse a promotion. A classroom teacher, Mrs. Richards has thought that moving into administration would give her an extra measure of professional respect as well as additional money. The Richards clan has long equated financial gain with success. She finally realizes that she *loves* teaching and that life is too short to spend it doing something she does not truly enjoy just for the sake of appearance. Eventually she is able to extend the same privilege to her children.

It takes longer for Mr. Richards to alter his mindset. But by Christmas of George's gophering year, George has won his father's respect. Although he had not clearly thought out the consequences of sabotaging the college application process, George has not complained about his life in the workforce. He has demonstrated to his father that when he accepts responsibility, he carries out the commitment. He has budgeted his time and money well. He has used his time-out to take stock of his values and goals. Thus, for Christmas, Mr. Richards offers George a new bike—one more suited for a delivery boy riding the streets during a Minnesota winter—and George realizes ". . . but what Dad was saying was more difficult for him that you'd have thought. He wasn't just offering me a gift; he was offering acceptance of the way I was" (*Gopher*, 200).

The Year of the Gopher ends on an upbeat note when Mr. Richards declares that the family probably already contains enough lawyers. In this novel Naylor has provided her young adult readers with a model—George—of how to move away from one's family in a positive way and how to use a developing sense of self and of empathy for others as the basis for action. As a review in *Booklist* describes the novel's strengths, "It is a welcome antidote to the compulsive, driving, college-entrance pressure exemplified in many nonfiction books."[9]

In addition, Naylor has provided a realistic portrait of the tensions that adolescent rebellion will cause in the family structure, but she has also shown the potential for growth of all concerned when the status quo is challenged. George does sometimes act foolishly—one of his friends almost drowns as a result of his insensitive teasing. George does sometimes engage in mock bravado/macho swaggering, and his conversations with his friends often reflect an adolescent sense of humor. His growth into selfhood is by no means complete by the end of the novel. But his appeal, and therefore his usefulness, to the adolescent reader engaged in a similar struggle for independence is undeniable.

George and the Richards family are very much part of the American mainstream middle class. They are derived from Naylor's participation as a parent in that lifestyle, as well as from her years of getting inside the head of the adolescent male, P. R. Tedesco. Naylor claims the easy rhythm and candor of the dialogue in George's story evolved from spending so many years articulating Tedesco's thoughts on life, parents, siblings, friends, God, and the future. Also, the scenes between George and Maureen resemble very closely scenes out of short stories originally published in Sunday school papers, such as those between Doug and Lorraine in "Starting Over."[10]

The real impetus for *The Year of the Gopher* surfaced during a cocktail party conversation she overheard. Engaged in an animated discussion—with Naylor seated between them—were a doctor and a woman whose brother had attended medical school. The woman's brother had left medical school to earn a Ph.D. in psychology and was now practicing in that field. But the woman, reports Naylor, was asking the doctor to visit her mother, who was "beside herself with grief" over her son's career choice. The son came from a long line of medical doctors, and his decision to become a psychologist instead had caused a great deal of pain in the family. Naylor asked the woman, "Is your brother happy?" She replied, "Of course, he's happy. What does that have to do with anything?" Naylor says that she felt as if she were in the "twilight zone," and she continued to think about this overheard conversation:

> I just kept thinking about it, and I *still* think about it. I've seen it in my sons' friends whose parents seem to have decided long ago what they would be, and I thought about how this situation is such an interesting thing for teens to have to deal with.

Naylor also admits that some of the Richards' behavior is derived from her own. At one point in childhood, a Richards child experimented with baking soda and vinegar on the front sidewalk. Almost immediately, the parents rushed out to buy him a chemistry set. Jeri asks the difference between a violin and viola; her mother gives her six years of piano lessons. Naylor says, "Well, that was me, more or less."[11] Like Mr. and Mrs. Richards, Naylor and her husband had to learn to trust their son's judgment about his academic future. Michael finished his first year of college with a C average and announced that he wanted to slow down the pace, take fewer courses a semester, and get better grades while also learning about life in other ways. Naylor reports, "Like the chorus in a Greek tragedy, we gave him dire warnings: all his friends would graduate ahead of him, we said, and with them gone, he might lose his motivation and not finish college at all."[12]

Michael held firm to his decision. He graduated within his own established time frame, *ahead* of all his friends, and with a 3.2 average. Naylor says, "What we had given was totally worthless advice." In *The Year of the Gopher* it takes George's parents a while, but they ultimately come to respect his ability to make his own choices. Their counterpart in the humorous "Alice" books is Aunt Sally, who always wants to help but never realizes that her outdated view of the world prevents her from offering Alice any truly valuable advice.

Send No Blessings—Moving Beyond the Limits of the Family's Vision

Beth Herndon, in *Send No Blessings* (1990; hereafter cited as *Blessings*), is similar to George in her need to pull away from her family in order to determine her identity and her own path through life. Because Beth's parents are members of the rural poor, however, her circumstances are quite different.

The Herndons live in a double-wide trailer on the outskirts of a very small West Virginia town. Beth's mother cleans rooms at the local motel, her father works as the grill man for a diner, and Beth contributes to the family till by making artificial flowers that the motel owner arranges for sale—a task her mother sometimes shares. The oldest of the eight children in the family, Beth spends a large part of her day outside school taking care of the others and working around the home.

In spite of their economic situation, Beth's family is a loving, caring one, and through junior high school she has been reasonably happy with her lot. Before turning 15 and entering tenth grade, she has not thought a great deal about the possibility that she might have a different kind of life. But at the beginning of *Send No Blessings,* Beth starts high school. The school bus picks her up right in front of the trailer, and she hears the other bus riders as they express their disbelief that a family of 10 actually lives in it. As in other books, Naylor uses a description of the physical environment to demonstrate an impending change in her character's life. Beth reflects on how pretty the setting for the trailer had always seemed, surrounded by maple trees and evergreens, below the cliff and near a beautiful river, under a beautiful West Virginia sky. Now, however, Beth wonders why her eyes had never

> focused on the Crisco can holding up one corner of the dilapidated porch her father had built, or the old refrigerator standing outside in the rain? The torn sheets of plastic over the windows . . . ?

Now, she could

> hear what she had tuned out before, . . . feel the kinds of things that made her silent now around the house. Her own little world at the foot of the cliff had developed a crack, and others were looking in. (*Blessings*, 5–6)

Having begun to look at her family and home with new eyes, Beth also begins to examine her future with new care. When her father assumes she can take a day off from school to finish an order of flowers, she realizes how important school has become in her life. Overhearing her father telling her mother that the manager of the diner is willing to hire Beth as a full-time waitress once she turns 16 in a few short months, she knows she is going to have to battle for what she wants. She resolves, "I'm not leaving school when I'm sixteen" and engraves the word "not" on the cover of her notebook. At the same time, she imagines her father challenging her decision, "You saying no to me, girl?"—and knows "somehow she'd have to get up the courage to say yes" (*Blessings*, 17).

Beth's father is not the only obstacle she will have to face in her struggle to determine what kind of a future she wants and how she will achieve it. School does not come easily to her. There is constant turmoil in her home, so that doing homework is difficult; after working for hours on her flowers, she studies late at night by flashlight under the bedcovers so as not to awaken her sister and to prevent her father from knowing what she is doing.

There are no reference books in the house, and staying late to use the school library is difficult for transportation reasons. Beth does, however, earn fairly consistent Cs, but the A+ she makes in typing—her first ever—shows her that she has the potential to do more with her life than take orders at the diner. Her father's reaction to her report card hurts her deeply. He makes no comment on the grade, merely stating that if she cannot do better in her other courses she should quit school. Beth realizes that for some time her father has been unable to offer her praise of any sort. Instead, he finds fault with almost everything she does, and she begins to wonder what she has done to cause her formerly loving father actively to dislike her. Their relationship is strained still further when Beth comes to realize that her father cannot read and thus feels locked out of the sorts of opportunities his daughter can envision.

Then Harless Prather enters the picture. At almost 23, he is seven years Beth's senior. He drives a truck, delivering bread and rolls in the region, and he is looking for someone with whom to share his life. He and Beth meet when Mr. Herndon, ill with the flu, asks Harless to drive the Herndon brood for their trick-or-treating on Halloween. Harless does not seem to mind the chaos created by Beth's siblings. He takes it in stride and treats them all to a visit to a restaurant complete with "paper menus." The Herndon family has never eaten out anywhere except, upon rare occasions, at Burger King. Not only does Harless seem comfortable with the children, he and Beth feel at ease talking to each other, even about their dreams for the future. By the end of the evening, Beth finds that she hopes she will see Harless again.

Harless and Beth begin dating. She enjoys knowing that Harless cares for and about her. Craving affection, she responds to his praise of her looks, her way with her siblings, her conversation. Her body also responds to his, and within a very short time, Beth has to determine how far she can and should let herself go. The temptation for her is to say yes to Harless in every way—and to let him take her away from the trailer and the demands of being the eldest child, from the anger of her father, from the image she sees in her mother's tired face of what the future in the trailer holds.

Beth's developing conviction that she not only can but must carve out a different sort of life stands in sharp contrast to her mother's acceptance of the poverty and back-breaking chaos of the Herndon household. Beth is devastated to learn her mother is expecting child number nine, and she works up the courage to mention the idea of birth control. But Mrs. Herndon is adamant; children are blessings sent from God, and as long as God sees fit to keep extending the Herndon family, she will not complain. Beth's perspective is also more clearly delineated because Naylor contrasts it with that of Gerry, Beth's next younger sister, who feels good about herself only when she is with a young man and who therefore becomes sexually active—and pregnant—while barely a teenager.

Beth's self-esteem gets a boost from her typing teachers, who are impressed with her natural feel for the keyboard, and with her determination to improve her spelling and composing skill. They award her an unsolicited scholarship to a three-week career-planning seminar, and Beth heads to the state university after finally winning her father's approval in an ending deemed to weaken the plot overall.[13] Nonetheless, the tension between Beth and her father, the "realistic and moving depiction of rural poverty,"[14] and the "painful honesty"[15] of Beth's struggles won *Send No Blessings* a place on *Booklist's* "Best Books for Young Adults" list for 1991.[16]

There is much that is autobiographical in this novel about a young woman searching for an identity that will transcend the one provided by her family situation. Naylor certainly experienced the tension arising from trying to maintain both her individuality and the family equilibrium. In *Crazy Love* she notes that her family were "master detectives" of everyone's feelings but their own, able to read others' facial expressions and determine the slightest hint of disapproval written there (*Crazy Love*, 17).

In addition, the idea that one could succeed by working harder than others was frowned upon by the adults in Naylor's family. Success could be attributable only to God, a great teacher, or a relative. Thus Naylor found that she and the other children in the family were, like Beth, "ravenous" for praise (*Crazy Love*, 18).

The theme of the child's longing for adult recognition is one played out in many of Naylor's books for younger readers. Jed, in the older (1971) *Wrestle the Mountain*, is a younger (sixth-grade), male version of Beth in many ways. His father, like Beth's, sees only one possible future for his son: Jed is destined, from his parents' point of view, to follow the family tradition of working in the coal mines of rural West Virginia. But, like Evie from *A String of Chances*, Jed has a desire to make things. Like Beth, he has a talent that, with guidance, could evolve into a marketable skill and thus be the basis for an alternative set of life choices. His artistic ability as a sculptor in wood wins him an opportunity to leave his hometown and explore the wider world, just as Beth's typing skill wins her a similar chance to make her own path.

Beth's struggle to find a sense of identity that is her own, that is not dependent on her relationship with a man, is one that Naylor conveys eloquently because she too wrestled with the same problem:

> A man. The very word held the connotation of something marvelous, much to be desired. . . . to be so attractive that a *man* would want to spend his life with me had always been an unspoken hope. To fail was to be nothing, for a woman without a man was pathetic. . . .
>
> All I knew was that it was imperative to keep my husband, psychotic or not, because I had little self image apart from him. (*Crazy Love*, 54–55)

Having found the seeds of her own self-worth and of a positive self-image through success as a writer, Naylor is able to show her readers characters such as Beth—and even the younger Alice—who work conscientiously to believe in their own inherent worth and to develop a solid identity *before* committing to a relationship.

Furthermore, Naylor knew, personally, the importance for a child of finding an adult mentor. Because she had teachers who praised her skill, Naylor found an identity at school as a writer. Would the teenaged Naylor ever have pursued the career that now seems so right for her if her Sunday school teacher had not suggested she submit a story for publication? What choices would

Beth have made had Miss Talbot not provided a contrasting image of womanhood than the one her mother afforded her?

In the books discussed in the previous chapter, the young adults confront issues arising primarily from within family structures. They exhibit maturity and wisdom in establishing independent personalities as a basis for engaging in the world. Young readers can emulate these behaviors. But, clearly, young adults interact with the world at large as well as with the microcosm of their families. In chapter 5, we will explore Naylor's recurring theme of decision making.

5. Defining the Self in the World at Large: *When Rivers Meet, Making It Happen, No Easy Circle, Walking through the Dark, Night Cry, The Dark of the Tunnel,* and *Unexpected Pleasures*

Whereas some of the young people in the books discussed in the previous two chapters are growing up in homes in which resources are limited, others are financially secure. What they share is a need to craft a personal identity, regardless of their family situation. However, in other titles for young adults, Naylor focuses on the strategies young people—especially those who are not from privileged homes—use to solve problems and moral dilemmas that occur when their values conflict with those of a larger society. In addition, young people without a family structure in place—who are nevertheless trying to define themselves—are also Naylor's subjects. In all of these titles, Naylor's young protagonists make decisions that challenge established norms. The plot tensions in these books center on the young people's need to find both the courage and the resources to make their decisions.

When Rivers Meet and *Making It Happen*—
When Beliefs and Values Clash with
Accepted Behavioral Norms

In *The Craft of Writing the Novel* (1989; hereafter cited as *Craft*), Naylor states that a theme might be a "universal truth that may be difficult to accept" and continues by saying that the theme of a story *has* to be personally meaningful to the author (*Craft*, 19). Of plot, she writes, "Something must happen that makes this week or this month or this year in the life of your main character different from any other time of life, or why write about it at all?" (*Craft*, 36). She goes on to elaborate,

> Somewhere fairly close to the beginning of your book, the reader must sense that there is a question mark hanging over your protagonist, . . . that there is a decision or a choice to be made . . . and that upon this decision or choice rests the futures or fortunes of several other characters as well. (*Craft*, 39)

It is interesting to examine Naylor's first novels in light of these statements about the craft of writing. As previously mentioned, when asked about her very early novel, *When Rivers Meet* (1968; hereafter cited as *Rivers*), Naylor expresses her dismay at agreeing to tackle the assignment for this book given to her by a committee at Friendship Press. One of the main characters is an Ethiopian, a young man from the royal, ruling family of that country. He comes to a town in the Midwest at the invitation of Pastor Lee, who wants his congregation to learn "what it's like to be truly Christian and humanitarian in small ways" (*Rivers*, 60), so that they will have a scaffold on which to build when tackling larger social issues.

As Naylor notes, today she would never attempt to write about such a character. But Alemu serves basically as a catalyst. His presence in the town sparks events, creates discussion, and causes other characters to reflect on their values. Naylor does not have to round out Alemu's character, and she has very little need to deal with details of Ethiopian life and culture. She followed her own advice well, using Alemu's arrival in the home of the Chapmans, his hosts, to create the disequilibrium necessary for the ultimate growth of the protagonist, Kenny. Furthermore, Naylor's passion for her theme—the role of the church in challenging the status quo—helps develop a story that, in spite of its excesses and sometimes too-quick solutions, still has relevance in a society continuing to wrestle with racial tensions.

Alemu is the victim of the racial prejudice that Paul Kern, a black student and friend of Kenny's, has felt most of his life. Naylor uses Alemu's status as an outsider to provide Paul with a sounding board for his reflections on race relations in the United States. Paul tells Alemu

> It's a big, rich country with plenty of opportunity if you're white, like Kenny. For the Kerns, it's a rat hole. . . .
> We drop out of high school? We're dumb. We go to college? We're only trying to be better than anyone else. There's only one thing Whitey wants—a subservient black savage he can wipe his feet on. . . .
> The church is the breeding place of hypocrisy, Alemu. Brotherly love? Everybody loves his own color—that's the rule. Christians are cowards. (*Rivers*, 25–26)

Considering the publication date of this novel, 1968, and the fact that it was commissioned by a Christian publishing house, Naylor's words demonstrate clearly her willingness to deal with social issues. In *Rivers*, she shows the need for Christians to take a real stand and to operate on those values of equality and fairness that underpin Christian doctrine. One evening, Paul, Alemu, and the Chapman daughter, Leslie, are stopped by police while walking to a bus stop. The assumption of the police officers is that the two young men are somehow taking advantage of the girl. When he arrives at the police station, Mr. Chapman is incensed. But the police maintain that a) the Chapmans should have told them that they were hosting a royal visitor from Ethiopia who would be walking in their part of town at night, and b) the Chapmans should not let their daughter walk about in the company of Paul even with Alemu along as well. The police insist that

Paul take a bus to his home, refusing to allow Mr. Chapman to drive him there.

Mrs. Chapman has trouble understanding why Mr. Chapman is so troubled by the attitude of the police toward Paul. "He must be used to it," she says. Mr. Chapman's conscience is beginning to stir, however, and he points out, "That's just it! It's another in a long string of abuses. And here we sit, allowing something like this to go unprotested" (*Rivers*, 93).

The tension in the community escalates even further. The latent prejudice against anyone perceived to be outside the mainstream erupts in anti-Semitic activity during the Jewish holidays. Some students and their parents do not like the fact that a Jewish student is head of the student council. Once again Naylor uses the metaphor of water to indicate the severity of the problem of attitude and values affecting the entire town. The river flowing through the town grows "angry."

With the river rising at an alarming rate, the levees that hold the water in check begin to break. The town rushes to stem the breach. The effort is successful at the north end of town, but the workers run out of sandbags before the river crests, and Paul Kern knows that his neighborhood will be drastically affected when the river reaches its height and pours through the streets. The river wins this particular battle. During the long fight to protect the town, everyone works together toward a common goal. Paul demonstrates a courage and a humanitarian outlook that undercut his surface cynicism. He rescues a student, a boy who has been particularly hateful to him, when he falls into the raging water. Not everyone understands the significance of these two events of the night, but Alemu notes that, at least for some individuals, the chance to be a part of something larger than their own blind hate has had a positive effect.

Building on the flood experience, Kenny decides someone has to be an advocate for change, and he has the courage to be that someone. With the support of his father and his minister, Kenny lobbies to organize a series of panel discussions cosponsored by various churches and religious groups, on hot topics, ranging from race to mental health. By asking people who have been rather hostile to Alemu and others perceived as different to take charge of specific tasks, such as organizing the refreshments or arranging for publicity, Kenny and company provide a sense of ownership for these individuals that helps them feel more positive about the possibility of changing the status quo.

Nevertheless, the novel does not end on an entirely happy note. Kenny is fired from his part-time job because his boss is afraid that shop customers will not want to be served by someone perceived as a social activist. Kenny says he is sorry to have lost his position, "but not half as sorry as I'd be if I backed out. . . . Once you start selling little pieces of yourself, there's just nothing left" (*Rivers*, 153).

To the extent that Kenny and other characters offer such insights in what sometimes is a fairly didactic fashion, this very early novel, which was never even reviewed, has less to recommend it than Naylor's later works. But the characterizations are consistent, the plot moves along in a steady way toward a climax that clearly demonstrates that change in society begins with changes in individuals. Naylor intertwines important themes, such as the definition of courage, the importance of community, and the role of religion as a basis for social action.

In *Making It Happen* (1970), Naylor tackles similar themes. Here she achieves a more realistic sense of voice for three young high school men who struggle more than Kenny does to figure out what it is about societal norms that confuses them. When John meets M. L. Gifford, he knows he has found a kindred spirit. John says "Hi." Gifford says, "When." John asks, "When is what?" Gifford proceeds to explain that there are no absolutes in his mind, arguing that words like "hi," "when," "what," or even "butter" are arbitrary in meaning. John loves this exchange and decides that Gifford, new to the school, is "something definitely not of this world—the world of button-down collars and ball point pens" (*Making It Happen*, 7).

Together John and Gifford decide to challenge the school principal, who seems to believe that all high school students should want to become members of corporate America. The principal has, for quite some time, dictated that certain days will be "dress-up" days. John and Gifford organize their fellow students into undermining these events. They announce that if dress-up days are mandated, the students will boycott, without warning, some particular element of the school cafeteria's offerings. The cafeteria would, under these conditions, never know how much to order of any particular item, and its financial situation would be dramatically affected.

The principal gives in, but John and Gifford still feel restless. They want to challenge "complacency, monotony, shallowness, convention—you name it" (*Making It Happen*, 59), but they really have no idea how to do so. Then Lee Prather arrives on the scene. As the first African American in the school, Lee's mere presence challenges accepted norms, and it is no surprise that John and Gifford want to become Lee's friends—especially since they know their parents would not be pleased. Lee is not about to be used by them, however. He makes it very clear that if they are only befriending him to make a statement, he will not participate. The three boys work out their friendship. They next decide to set off the fire alarms at the school, and then they run away together in a misguided effort to show their parents and the school authorities that they "were special somehow . . . that beneath the labels [they] shared a common soul" (*Making It Happen*, 111). Naylor draws a clear portrait of the confusion of adolescents struggling with a desire to rebel, even when it is difficult for them to articulate the nature of their dissatisfaction.

In a garage on the "wrong" side of town, the boys hole up with few provisions. Lee's brother Paul finds them and brings them both food, other supplies, and his own brand of advice about their situation. Paul, who has faced a lot of prejudice head on as an African American college student on a campus where he stands out as very different, tells them they have to decide if what they believe in is worth the effort of a fight. He says,

> Don't sweat the little things, that's my philosophy, I guess. If somebody says I've got to wear a tie . . . that's what I do. . . . But if somebody tells me I've got to segregate, . . . then I've got

steam, see. . . Folks'll clear out of the way for an engine if it really steams." (*Making It Happen*, 113)

Eventually, the boys return home. Gifford's parents decide to move away. John's and Lee's parents make an effort to listen to their sons and try to understand their friendship and their need to make some of their own decisions. As a result, John and Lee, still feeling their way, begin to recognize that they cannot just try to shake things up for the sake of doing so. They begin to inch their way toward a clearer sense of what they stand for and of how to go about working toward change. They accept an invitation to be part of the student council and to act in an advisory capacity to the principal, sharing their insights about what changes the students want and need in school policy to reflect changes in society at large.

Like *When Rivers Meet*, *Making It Happen* received little critical notice. But more than the earlier book, it demonstrates Naylor's ability to find a consistent voice and to define characters who are in the throes of self-definition. There are elements in the book that are more fully explored in later titles. John is, in many ways, an earlier version of George from *The Year of the Gopher*. He even has the same "lucky sperm" thought as George. Also, like George, he rebels against his perceptions of what his family wants for him in the future. Ultimately, however, John is more like Kenny. He attempts to define himself by taking a stand on a serious societal issue: race relations. He learns something about the nature of true leadership in the process, and he will be an agent for change within the school, a realistic scope of influence within which a young person might operate.

Walking through the Dark, Night Cry, and *The Dark of the Tunnel*— When External Forces Affect the Status Quo

Ruth Wheeler, in *Walking through the Dark* (1976; hereafter cited as *Walking*), learns a lesson different from that experienced by John, Lee, and Kenny. When her story begins, just prior to the start of the Great Depression, she is very comfortable with the status quo. She is a somewhat self-absorbed, self-centered young woman who accepts a certain standard of living as her due. When Mrs. Wheeler drags Ruth and her younger sister along on yearly visits to the home of their former housekeeper, Annie, Ruth is habitually disgusted at what she perceives as the woman's slovenly ways. Ruth cannot accept the fact that when there is no running hot water, standards of personal hygiene suffer, and she is horrified by Annie's odor as well as by her blackened teeth, the result of her inability to afford dental care and a balanced diet. When her mother gives food to a beggar who knocks on the door, Ruth is appalled by the way in which he stuffs the sandwich and pie into his mouth as if afraid they will disappear if he cannot consume them quickly enough.

At age 14, Ruth spends her time wondering what it is like to kiss a boy, trying to figure out a way to help her exceptionally tall friend Kitty meet basketball players and planning her future as a wonderful teacher. Her desire to go to college to become an educator is based on her sense of the dramatic. She sees herself surrounded by adoring students who do not want to leave the room when the class ends.

Unfortunately for Ruth, her father loses his job as the economic turmoil of the Depression hits the furniture store he has managed. At first, Ruth is impatient with her dad. Why can't he just find another job? She tunes out his stories of his efforts to gain other employment, focusing instead on figuring out how to attract the attention of Clyde, a young man from school. In a book written more than a decade before the "Alice" series, Naylor begins to hone her craft in portraying the inner life of girls on the brink of womanhood. She writes,

> Now the chief activity on Saturday afternoons was an hour's debate with Kitty discussing strategy, followed by a leisurely, well-rehearsed stroll to Clyde's neighborhood and surveillance from a distance of the house in which he lived. Saturday afternoon was, in short, taken up with the *awful* hope of being discovered. (*Walking*, 59)

Clyde and Ruth finally do get together and go to the movies for Ruth's first date. Naylor's description of how Clyde slips his arm around Ruth's shoulder, of how they both almost stop breathing from the intensity of just this tiny bit of unaccustomed intimacy, and of how their hands then find each other, communicating in the darkness almost like separate entities, is right on target. Ruth, like many young women in the same situation, feels that even if nothing good ever happens to her again, this one moment in the movie theater would make up for it.

What Ruth does not know is that she is, in fact, destined to experience little joy in the near future. Christmas rolls around, and the stockings contain only oranges and walnuts. Ruth has to stuff paper in her shoes because there are holes in her soles and there is no money for new ones. She and her younger sister sneak, embarrassed, through the cover of night to deliver the laundry her mother is forced to take in to help make ends meet. Her father takes a job selling matches and shoelaces door-to-door.

At first Ruth cannot accept the situation. She screams at her mother, "Just not starving doesn't matter! Just being alive doesn't count!" (*Walking*, 70–71). Gradually, however, Ruth comes to believe that surviving and keeping the family together sometimes *is* the only thing that matters. She becomes aware of her mother's courage in doing whatever is necessary to keep her daughters alive in the face of increasing poverty. She recognizes her father's continual willingness to take whatever job he can as an act of courage. Always rather strong-willed, Ruth begins to feel a grim determination not to let the Depression break her. She develops a pride that comes from doing what has to be done— including doing the laundry of those more fortunate—to help her family survive. The next time her mother takes her to visit Annie, the stench of Annie's poverty stacked against the evidence that Annie, now very poor, has been raising vegetables that she shares with others, touches Ruth in a new way. She recognizes Annie as being as determined and courageous as her own parents.

Naylor shows Ruth maturing in several ways. Readers see her responding differently to Annie. She takes a seat in Annie's house rather than remaining outside as she has done in the past. We see her walking with her chin high to the soup kitchen to get food for the family. We see her trying her best to make life easier for her younger sister, to cheer up Kitty, whose height depresses her, to befriend Michael, a lodger taken in by the Wheelers to help make ends meet. We see her continuing to work at her studies because of a growing commitment to become a teacher for more altruistic reasons.

When Ruth learns that Clyde has retracted his invitation to take her to an important school dance because he has been able to win the attention of a wealthy young woman, the reader feels for her. Naylor demonstrates her ability to capture the real agony of adolescent humiliation in this passage:

> [Ruth] felt as though her whole body had turned to ice. For a moment she felt she couldn't catch her breath and then she was weak all over.... She knew now why it was she whom he had chosen to walk around the park with on weekends: because she was poor and would never expect any better. He couldn't afford anything else ... Ruth had been better for his ego than no girl at all. But now he didn't need her. (*Walking*, 153)

Like the response of Naylor's own family to her first husband's illness and the grim circumstances related to caring for him, Ruth's family helps her survive through small, quiet kindnesses. Eventually Ruth is able to model her own behavior on that of her mother and father. For instance, she plays matchmaker, arranging for Michael to take her friend Kitty to the dance for which she herself no longer has a date, and as she reflects on the state of her emotions, she is "pleased that she was capable of caring for somebody else when she felt so lonely inside. Compassion and empathy. That's what she admired in Miss Harley [her teacher]. Was she beginning to develop it, too?" (*Walking*, 158).

Miss Harley serves Ruth in the way that many of Naylor's other protagonists are well served by adults outside their families. Like the nurse in *The Keeper* or Mrs. Plotkin in the Alice books, it is Miss Harley who recognizes that Ruth is becoming a better person and who is able to tell her so in language that she can understand and accept. She advises Ruth to use all the disappointments and heartbreaks of the Depression years as food on which to grow—and she notes that, in similar fashion, as a teacher Ruth should be open to learning from, and growing with, every student in her care. From Miss Harley, Ruth learns the truth about the profession of teaching:

> Most of the time the students aren't reaching out to me, the way it seems. I have to reach out to them, to go after them, to capture their imaginations by force. It's not enough, see, for them to accept me or listen to me or like me. I've got to accept *them*, and this means not only the eager students, like you, but the slow ones, the homely ones, the ones that mispronounce and fidget, the ones who never change their socks. They're all students of mine, and somehow I have to reach them all. That's the hard part. That's the challenge. (*Walking*, 201)

After the dance, which Ruth, Kitty, and Michael attend together—he taking *both* girls as dates—Ruth lets go of a bouquet of beautiful blue balloons her friends have given her. As she watches them soar into the sky, she experiences the same sort of optimism about the future that Nick in *The Keeper*, George in *The Year of the Gopher*, and Alice in so many of her titles feels. The reader believes that Ruth *will* be able to survive her family's situation, to rise above her circumstances, and to serve others with conviction and passion.

Walking through the Dark was not a hit the first time Naylor sent it to Jean Karl, her editor. Based on her personal experiences, Karl voiced concern that the details of Depression life in Chicago were not accurate. Karl also told Naylor that Ruth had to develop more fully if she were to capture the empathy of potential readers. In *How I Came to Be a Writer*, Naylor recalls that she thought a great deal about why Ruth was not more fully realized in the draft she first showed Karl. Eventually she decided that she did not like Ruth; she perceived Ruth as shallow and selfish. But finally Naylor realized, "even selfish people have times of generosity and certainly feel fear and hope" (*How I Came*, 78).

Once Naylor had this revelation, she was able to fill out the details of Ruth's personality. Ruth became, in the process, more sympathetic, and the book came alive, although some reviewers were only lukewarm in their response to the novel. Ironically, given Karl's initial comments, Ruth Stein wrote in *Language Arts*, "The author's lavish care [with historical detail] makes a depressing time in history come alive."[1] But Stein and other reviewers still did not find Ruth's story compelling enough. As Lillian Gerhardt wrote in *School Library Journal*, "Poverty transcended is interesting, even uplifting. Poverty endured is dull. The Wheelers endure."[2]

However, other reviewers saw the book as both a well-drawn character study of a young woman who manages to transcend her circumstances and of a nation struggling to survive in difficult times. A review in *Horn Book* praised Naylor's ability to juggle a presentation of the "normal vicissitudes of adolescent life" with a realistic portrait of a sad time in the country's history.[3] The book was advocated as a useful curriculum tool by other reviewers.[4] Regardless of what others had to say, working on this book proved an important process for Naylor because she realized that *she* had to care about her main characters or she would be unable to convince her readers to do so. In *The Craft of Writing the Novel,* Naylor draws on her experiences with characters like Ruth to tell budding young authors,

> The author can become all these people, the horrible as well as the wonderful, because he, too, has moments of arrogance, of cowardice, of being mean-spirited as well as sadistic. And by tapping that vein within ourselves, however shameful, however hidden, we may expand upon it, dwell upon it, magnify it there on paper until it is *our* meanness, *our* arrogance, *our* selfishness that we are writing about and we are drawing from our own experiences. (*Craft*, 53)

Using the "what if" formula to help her generate this novel, Naylor says she wrote the story because while our experience was that we seemed to be poorest about the time I was born, and gradually our financial situation improved year by year, I realized how little it affected me to be poor when I was in kindergarten and first grade, and how much more important it was to finally have some money for clothes by the time I was a teenager. I wondered what it would be like for a teenage girl to be used to a fairly comfortable life and then, one by one, have to give things up.[5]

Night Cry (1984) won the Edgar Allen Poe Award for Best Juvenile mystery. Also from a poor family, protagonist Ellen is a much more inherently sympathetic character than Ruth. Early in the novel, Naylor shows Ellen in action, practicing when alone in her home to be "Ellen Stump, News Reporter," doing chores like collecting eggs from the red hen, and helping her father "make do" on his limited income. Her father wonders if he should give her a different sort of life and suggests they trade their rural isolation for a condominium in town. Ellen and her father have a good-natured relationship:

Ellen rested her head on her hand and made a teasing face. "With a swimming pool, I suppose?"
"Sure. Tennis court, too."
"Don't have any bathing suit."
"We'll get you one."
"Never held a tennis racket in my life."
"Time you learned."
"Huh. We go getting all fancy like that, Dad, and I got to have me a coming-out party like the girls in Jackson do."
"What kind of party is that?"
"You know—where they all wear long dresses and their fathers walk them around a ballroom and introduce them to everybody."
"*Introduce 'em?*" Joe said. "Where they been all this time, those girls? Locked in the basement?"
They laughed together. (*Night Cry*, 5)

Ellen accepts her life and enjoys its rhythms and routines. Naylor, as in her other books, uses a description of the landscape to convey a character's state of mind. In the following passage, readers learn how Ellen has viewed her situation, and they get a sense of the change that is imminent:

> [T]he land was enclosed by a wall of vine, so dense and dark that trees leaned with its weight. It matted the underbrush, making an impenetrable net of leaves and branches. For as long as Ellen could remember, the closed-in feeling had given her a kind of security, defining her boundaries, setting a limit on where she need go. But there were other times, especially in the last year or two, when she had felt uncomfortably trapped, as though the familiar things that had brought such comfort before had turned on her sharply and become the wardens of her own prison. (*Night Cry*, 17)

As the plot unfolds, Ellen increasingly feels the oppressiveness of her situation, symbolized by the kudzu, and has to cut through her growing sense of suffocation by the familiar in order to take a stand in the world at large, in spite of her deep-seated fears. When her father goes off on a business trip, a stranger shows up on Ellen's porch. Having taken refuge in an abandoned house, he asks if he can exchange work for food for himself and his sick wife. Meanwhile, Ellen learns that the son of a wealthy actor, a hometown boy who made good and was determined to share his success with the community, has been kidnapped. She is scared that the stranger, Gerald, may be guilty, and so is fearful for her own safety. She also begins to question the veracity of her neighbor, Granny Bo, on whom the townspeople want to pin the crime. Then, as her fears grow, she begins to wonder if her father might be involved. He has always had dreams of "hitting it big," of making a huge sale and of having the money necessary for a more luxurious lifestyle.

Ellen gathers clues, among them a mysterious "night cry" that is cut off in the middle of its utterance, which finally convince her that Gerald is to blame. Ellen knows she has to take action. She actually sees Gerald and his wife packing their car and hears them talking about where they are heading with Jason, the actor's child. She sets a fire to distract the couple, runs into the house, and talks Jason into fleeing with her. Then she has to confront her deepest fear of all.

"Sleet" is the horse that threw Ellen's brother in the not too distant past, killing him quickly and leaving Ellen so alone. Ever since, Ellen has been terrified of Sleet, has been convinced he is evil and has the devil in him. She has not been able to bring herself even to feed him a treat or touch him, although she had been a good, and avid, rider. Ellen's father has told her, however, that the most important lesson to be learned about evil is that "There's always evil about. . . . What you got to learn is when to doubt and when to trust, and that's not something that comes easy" (*Night Cry*, 36).

Desperate to save herself and her young charge, Ellen recalls her father's words and decides she will have to trust Sleet, will have to draw on the relationship that existed between the horse and herself before her brother's death. She hides in Sleet's stall, knowing Gerald believes that she is too terrified of the animal to take refuge there, and begins trying to win Sleet's trust again. She croons to the horse, blows gently on his nostrils, speaks to him softly, and, in the process, comes to recognize that Sleet has been acting wild because he has been treated with so much fear of late. She begs the horse to help her, and, knowing it is the moment of truth, pulls Jason up onto the horse's back, mounts Sleet, and urges him into a gallop across the fields and away from the evil Gerald. She makes it safely, with the boy, to the sheriff.

It turns out that Gerald is really Sam Goff, out for revenge against the movie actor who had fired him years ago. He and his accomplice are apprehended; Ellen is a hero. She has learned a good deal about herself and her relationships and about the need for individuals to triumph over coincidences:

> Coincidence of place and time and weather on the day Billy died had caused her to change a horse once loved into a demon undeserving of charity or forgiveness. . . . resentment at her father's leaving had allowed Ellen to suspect the man she cared about more than anyone else in the world. (*Night Cry*, 146)

Ellen teaches the adolescent reader a good deal about the nature of heroism. As she talks with her father about how to spend the reward money, which will probably go to help with tuition at a junior college, she tells him she feels embarrassed, not heroic. She concedes, "Wasn't one ounce of courage in me, Dad. I was scared as a polecat up a tree over a river." Her father replies, "You were scared half out of your mind, but you went and did it anyways" (*Night Cry*, 151). Ellen goes on to confess to her father that, in the midst of everything, she had wondered if he were mixed up in the kidnapping. Her dad just hugs her close and says he will not leave her to travel on the road any more.

Naylor ends the book as she begins: with a description of the natural world surrounding Ellen. But now that Ellen is more at peace with herself, the countryside is no longer described in claustrophobic terms. Instead of seeing kudzu twining around every aspect of the landscape, Ellen sees a thrush's nest, hears the cry of a baby raccoon, sees buckberries that she will pick, and drinks in the fragrance of ripe plums, "the hint of a new September" (*Night Cry*, 153).

Night Cry has been praised for its sense of place, its use of description, and its use of "dialogue enriched by the backwoods dialect of a large cast of characters"[6] as well as for its plotting of a tension-filled mystery leading to an exciting climax and satisfying resolution.[7]

But the novel's real strength is in the characterization of Ellen. Like Alice, Ellen has no female role model. Also like Alice, she has a father, who, although often on the road, is a supportive, loving man. Readers see the characters and events of the novel through her eyes, and so feel the pain she feels when she begins to have doubts about her father. The absolute terror she feels toward Sleet, the way the familiarity of her home becomes threatening when the stranger intrudes and upsets her equilibrium, and the final sense of peace she attains when things are once more back on an even keel—although her life has been changed dramatically by the events of the story—are all so well described that the reader enters into her mind and heart.

Naylor is able to create such a believable character in such a believable setting because of her own childhood experiences in rural environments. Her Maryland grandparents were from the south, and her own father was born in Yazoo City, Mississippi. The cadence of the dialect in *Night Cry* echoes those of Naylor's family members. Also, Naylor knows quite a bit about what it is like to feel terrified and alone—and yet to do what has to be done to move forward, as she had to do when her first husband succumbed to paranoia. Even though Ellen is apparently not an autobiographical character, many of those aspects of her personality that make her appealing and empathetic to readers mirror much that is pure Naylor.

Craig Sheldon, in *The Dark of the Tunnel* (1985; hereafter cited as *Tunnel*), also exhibits characteristics that have their origins in Naylor's life history. Once again, Naylor applies her knowledge of rural mountain life to create a setting that influences plot events in significant ways. Like Nick from *The Keeper*, and like Naylor herself, Craig has to cope with the debilitating, and ultimately terminal, illness of a parent. Like Naylor—and Evie from *A String of Chances* and Beth from *Send No Blessings*—Craig is a "maker," a photographer. Like Naylor herself, and like Jed from *Wrestle the Mountain*, Craig will use his talents as an artist to make his way in the world. Like George from *The Year of the Gopher*, and like Naylor, Craig has to find the determination to confront significant adults in his life and to take a stand for something he believes.

A high school senior, Craig often visits a tunnel outside town that carries water from a canal through the mountain. He values the privacy it affords and uses it as a place to consider his future. Hoping to win a scholarship to a state university to study photography, he is not sure he can leave home even if he is offered the support. His father is dead, the result of a coal mining accident, and his mother is dying of cancer. Who will take care of his younger brother, Lonnie, if Craig goes off to school? What is it that is eating at Big Jim, the uncle with whom Craig and family have been living? And what has caused John Mott, nicknamed Cougar, to become such an unsociable hermit, which fascinates

Craig—and does Cougar know anything about what is worrying Big Jim?

The novel opens with a description of the fear that Craig—like Ellen—constantly faces because of his mother's illness. Photography provides him with one outlet for his fear, providing a measure of control over his environment and a way to sort out what he sees and hears in manageable fashion. In the Sheldon family, people keep their feelings to themselves, and "Craig was beginning to discover just how lonely that can be" (*Tunnel*, 43). What Craig and his mother, uncle, and younger brother all have to learn is that it is important to share emotions and to work together in the face of adversity. *The Dark of the Tunnel* is a novel about the nature of courage, about the importance of truth in relationships, and about the need for honest communication and collaboration in the face of external events that could otherwise destroy an individual.

The truth of this need comes home to Craig when the doctor finally tells him and his uncle that chemotherapy is not doing any good and that the tumor's growth is out of control. Craig has the unenviable task of telling Lonnie about their mother's condition. Lonnie responds with anger, calling Craig a liar, saying Craig had never indicated their mom would die.

> "I wasn't sure," Craig said miserably.
> "Yes, you *were*!" Lonnie screamed, furious. "You *all* knew she wasn't going to get better. Nobody would tell me. It scares me when no one wants to talk about things! . . ."
> It was natural to hope. Healthy, even. But he had done Lonnie no favor in ignoring the possibility that Mother would die. Even when possibility turned to probability, he had still passed out subtle reassurances and false hopes as though they were candy—by what was left unspoken as much as by what he had said. (*Tunnel*, 134)

Craig finally realizes that not only did Lonnie need to hear the truth in order to be able to accept it, but his mother also needs her sons to accept the reality of her condition. He reflects,

> Maybe what she needed most of all was not the false comfort
> that she was going to live, but the knowledge that after she was
> gone, she would still be loved and remembered—that she had
> made Jim's house a home for them and that her love of flowers
> and trees and sky had added beauty to their lives. . . . There
> came a time when you had to face up to the truth, a point at
> which you looked into the heart of the trouble and recognized
> just how bad it could be. Until then you couldn't begin to solve a
> problem; you couldn't even cope. Mom had been trying to get to
> that place all by herself, and it must have been the loneliest
> thing she'd ever done. (*Tunnel*, 135–36)

Craig's mother dies, and, like Nick and Naylor, Craig takes
refuge in the simple acts of daily routine. But the outside world
infringes on the family's efforts to find peace. Big Jim is in trouble with the people of the community because, acting as Chief of
Civil Defense, he has been struggling to garner cooperation for a
civil defense drill called for by the government. In theory, 1,500
people are supposed to leave their homes and seek shelter in
Craig's tunnel, while certain stores and gas stations stay open to
service their journey and while the roads clog with people from
neighboring towns who are also supposed to use it. As Jim says,
"Wouldn't take someone past the third grade to see that the
whole thing makes about as much sense as an umbrella in a bliz-
zard" (*Tunnel*, 174).

But Jim is reluctant to point out the inanities in the government's plan until Craig, who up to this point has silently tried to
support Jim's position, tells his uncle, "There's got to be a time,
somewhere in the beginning, when folks stand up and say no"
(*Tunnel*, 158).

Having learned a good deal about the need to confront problems
head-on from his mother's death, Craig is the one who devises a
plan: Jim should call together the appointed leaders for the mock
evacuation, and together they should write a letter to the governor expressing their concerns and their unwillingness to go along
with the plans. Because his uncle and some of his peers are not
comfortable, fluent writers, Craig volunteers to help write the letter. He says, "Maybe you have to say no to one thing before you

can say yes to something else. . . Maybe you can say, 'Don't make better bombs, make better ambassadors or something.' At least it's a place to start" (*Tunnel*, 175).

Big Jim and the others write the letter and send it off to the governor, but, meanwhile, Cougar has taken matters into his own hands. He steals five hundred pounds of dynamite and blows up part of the mountain and the tunnel, taking his own life in the process, as a protest against the government's plans. The fallacies of those plans show up in sharp relief when local people, seeking safety, panic in the wake of the explosion. After newspaper reporters note just how much more serious the situation would be in the event of a true civil defense emergency, Big Jim is called to the State House to discuss alternatives.

Naylor says she wrote *The Dark of the Tunnel* because

> although I am a fearful person, I'm an optimistic person. And I want to share that. . . . I was just furious at the government's scheme to send everyone out to the Paw-Paw Tunnel in the event of an attack—except the people who live around there. And it was just so absolutely ludicrous. The brochures that I got said that gas stations and shops would be open along the way. Imagine! In a missile attack! A kindergarten child would know this couldn't be—how could the government say these things?

Naylor wrote Craig's story to protest the situation, and she thanks her editor for recognizing that this book *had* to be written. She notes

> My editor probably realized this wasn't a great book, and it wouldn't be widely read, and as it turned out, shortly after it was published, the Cold War was winding down. But she was wise enough to know that if I'm that upset about something, I can't seem to function or concentrate on anything else until that feeling is out, and so she took the book.

The Dark of the Tunnel sold very few copies, but Naylor is satisfied. Telling Craig's tale allowed her to purge the anger and fear from her system. Like Craig, Naylor found that taking action, taking a stand, provided a feeling of release and a sense of hope about the future. In spite of poor sales, the novel was well received. Byrna J. Fireside, writing in *Horn Book,* calls it a "richly textured" tale of courage and awakening,[8] and Nancy P. Reeder, in *School Library Journal,* praises Naylor's adept characterization and her ability to show, without didacticism, through Craig's struggles, "that more can be accomplished by being truthful with others than by trying to protect either them or yourself."[9]

Naylor has been active in both civil rights and peace organizations, and she is able to describe accurately the commitment to taking a stand that Craig and his uncle both develop. As in the Alice books, Naylor manages to combine flashes of humor with attention to serious themes, and she achieves, in the end, an invitation for adolescents to follow Craig's lead and become involved in the events shaping their world.

No Easy Circle and *Unexpected Pleasures*— When the Family Structure Does Not Support the Adolescent's Needs

Craig, Ellen, and Ruth are lucky to have supportive family structures on which to lean when they find themselves challenging the status quo. But the main characters in both *No Easy Circle* (1972; hereafter cited as *Circle*) and *Unexpected Pleasures* (1986; hereafter cited as *Pleasures*) have to create themselves and operate in the world without the benefit of helpful family relationships, struggling to determine their values and beliefs on their own.

No Easy Circle derived from a news article Naylor clipped from *The Washington Post* that described the life of runaways, young adults living on the streets of Washington. Naylor was struck by the fact that although many of these young people came from "nice" homes and therefore had difficulty adjusting to life in the rough, others, regardless of those difficulties, chose to stay on the street. She began wondering what would happen if two girls, fast friends but with very different goals, were in the same story and one chose to leave home (*How I Came,* 64–65). Thus was born the story of Shelley and Pogo.

Naylor had trouble finding a title for Shelley's story. At one point it was called *From the Mad Scenes of Shelley Elizabeth Greer*; at other times it went by *Looking for Pogo, Circling the Circle*, and *In Pogo's Place*. The sales representatives at Follett decided, finally, that they would have to name the book themselves so that they could sell it. *No Easy Circle* captures the nature of the setting—the street life around Dupont Circle in Washington, D.C.—and it reflects the inherent disquiet Shelley feels both when she visits Pogo on the street and when she returns, full circle, to her own home.

Both of these high school students have, on the surface, good homes, but it quickly becomes apparent that the parents of both girls are, in effect, absent from their lives. Neither of the girls has a very solid sense of self, nor do they have role models for developing one. Together they have tried to figure out what the future holds and have tried to understand their world, although Pogo has always been more adventurous, at least in conversation, than Shelley. Shelley, as narrator, says, "Pogo and I talked about sex all the time. Everybody did. Pogo and I could talk about anything, and sex was her favorite topic. We used to sit on the porch swing before Mother got home from work and imagine what it would be like on our wedding nights" (*Circle*, 18). Pogo smokes, drinks, and has had more encounters with boys than Shelley, who is far less experienced. She is distressed to learn that her father assumes she has smoked marijuana:

> For fifteen years I'd been his daughter, but he didn't even know me. I mean, I'd never even smoked in my life, that's how worldly I was. The newspapers said that all high school students knew where to buy pot, but no one had interviewed me. I didn't know. The worst things I had ever done in my whole life were to drink some beer at Pogo's and let a boy put his hand under my sweater (*Circle*, 44).

Shelley's father lives far away, in the Southwest, and she seldom sees him. Her mother, who works, tends to ignore her; Shelley is uncomfortable with her mother anyway because she seems constantly to be involved with yet another new man.

Pogo's mother is an invalid who badgers her daughter continually about caring for her younger siblings. Pogo eventually decides she will be better able to become an individual if she runs away, and Shelley is devastated. She feels as though she has lost a part of herself. Since fifth grade the girls have shared every possible emotion, from fear to curiosity to insecurity, and it hurts her to think that Pogo can survive alone.

Shelley attempts to visit Pogo at the "Circle" and even tries out various aspects of Pogo's lifestyle, getting drunk with one of Pogo's housemates and visiting a fortune teller. She is approached by a priest who tries to save her from Pogo's fate, but she runs, literally, from what he has to offer just as she runs from Pogo's new way of being. When Pogo announces that she is pregnant, Shelley realizes that she and Pogo are, in fact, very different people. Pogo seems happy enough with her decision to thumb her nose at convention, but Shelley cannot follow in her footsteps and still "be comfortable" (*Circle*, 124) with herself. Nor can she follow the path walked by her parents, who are motivated by money and material possessions; her mother uses quick encounters with men to plug the gaps in her life that her possessions cannot fill. Shelley's search, therefore, is for a blueprint for her life, an image of her future self that will provide a sense of direction.

In this respect, Shelley is an early draft of Alice. Both girls are looking for a role model, a woman whose life they can emulate. As she does for Alice, Naylor provides Shelley with someone. Mrs. Klopman, a social worker, is, like Alice's teacher Mrs. Plotkin (even their names are similar), a physically large and unattractive woman. Like her counterpart, Mrs. Klopman has a large and generous heart and an ability to accept Shelley for who she is, coupled with a faith in her ability to define herself in positive ways. Mrs. Klopman does not provide easy answers, but she encourages Shelley to create her own set of values, much as Mrs. Plotkin supports Alice on her journey toward selfhood. And Mrs. Klopman teaches Shelley important lessons about accepting others. She tells Shelley that her mother just wants to be loved:

"Well," I finally said, "if going to bed with men she hardly knows is what she calls love, I guess we've got different names for it."

"Perhaps that's as close as she can get to love right now. All of us want things we don't have, and sometimes we settle for a lot less and pretend it's what we're looking for."

It began to hurt inside me, thinking about Mom that way— thinking about her needing love and not having it, and Dad . . . not knowing how to love either.

"I can't go back there and watch her make a mess of her life," I protested.

"But you don't have to make a mess of yours," she reminded. "That's all the further your responsibility goes. . . . You don't have to love her for it, or hate her either, Shelley. All you have to do is understand why she's doing it. Then it will be easier to forgive her mistakes." (*Circle*, 126–27)

Shelley is, in the end, able to forgive her mother and Pogo, and she begins to determine her stance on drug use, smoking, and sexuality.

As in the Alice books, one of the strengths of *No Easy Circle* is the sense of voice. Shelley couples an emotional intensity at times with the wry sense of humor Naylor later hones in the Alice series. Riding a bus on her way to her first gynecological exam, Shelley, who is very nervous about the upcoming experience, describes the journey: "The bus went rolling down Connecticut Avenue full of little old ladies going to Magruder's for lamb chops, and it suddenly occurred to me that all of them, at sometime in their lives, had probably had a physical exam, and they were still alive, eating lamb chops" (*Circle*, 9). This is the same sort of insight Alice might have.

Naylor admits that she *is* Shelley, which enhances her ability to capture the young woman's thoughts and feelings so well. She says in *How I Came to Be a Writer* that, just like Shelley, during her own teen years and on into her early twenties, she had little sense of self. Like Shelley, Naylor wanted to be liked, she wanted to be accepted by the group, and she wished desperately for a role model (*How I Came*, 64). Because of the credibility of both Shelley's character and of her adventures, this novel won mention in Beckman's "Junior Books Too Good to Miss" column in the *English Journal*.[10]

April Ruth of *Unexpected Pleasures* is quite different from Shelley, but she, too, has a wonderfully distinctive voice and she, too, is faced with the need to figure out what she believes and how she wants to live her life without the benefit of familial support. Naylor aimed this book at an adult audience; hence it is more complex in its craft than her novels written specifically for young adults. "Written with an ear for idiom, an eye for comedy and a heart that delights in the graces and foibles of its two protagonists, this unlikely love story unites April Ruth Bates, 16-year-old sister of the town's two classiest prostitutes, with Foster Williams, a Chesapeake Bay bridge-builder twice her age."[11] Naylor alternates point of view, letting April Ruth present her version of events through first-person narration, but shifts to third-person limited when the less verbal, more reserved Foster's perspective is given.

Town do-gooders persuade Foster, 32, to marry April Ruth in order to save her from her alcoholic father and her notorious sisters. April, naive and fearful, agrees. She has known Foster all her life and thinks life with him will be better than life in foster care, and she is, in fact, eager to escape the demoralizing circumstances of her father's trailer home. The appeal to adolescents comes from the fact that the novel is both a love story and a coming-of-age story. As April Ruth and Foster struggle to create a life for themselves, each one has to examine his or her values, hopes, and dreams.

At first, life is good. Foster brings home a decent living, and he is an upright man. Quite limited in experience with women, Foster is tender and gentle with the girl and delights in her openness to the wonders of the world. Foster cooks and cleans; April Ruth plants vegetables. She discovers a knack for gardening, reflecting, "Seems like I had a natural sympathy for anything trying to grow, make something of itself" (*Pleasures*, 107).

But the couple faces growing pains. April Ruth eventually feels confined by Foster's attention; she wants a sense of individuality and knows she cannot be a good partner in their marriage if she lacks this distinctiveness—and if Foster refuses to recognize her ability to contribute to a true partnership. When Vinnie, their dog, is killed, Foster becomes accusatory and shows a darker side of himself that scares April into running away. She gets a job at a diner, takes up with another man, becomes pregnant with his child, rejects her sisters' lifestyle, and copes with the murder of one of them. But when Foster, eaten up with concern and anger, slips while working high above the bay and is hospitalized, April, now more secure about what she wants and who she is, goes to see him.

Eventually the two are reunited. They have discovered, independently, that they share a set of values that separates them from some of their peers. April reflects,

> "We make room in our lives for things we don't expect. We don't give up and we don't break down, and except for me leaving Foster that one time, we don't run away, neither." (*Pleasures*, 260)

The courage of Foster and April Ruth is the courage required to face whatever happens in life and to do their best to "make room for the unexpected," both the difficulties, like Foster's serious accident, and the pleasures. They learn the courage required to be a true couple. At the very end of the book, April makes Foster pledge in writing that he will share *all* of his life, the problems and the joys with her; she makes him say "how I got as much right to share [his] problems as I got to share [his] bed" (*Pleasures*, 269).

Naylor says of April Ruth,

> I loved April Ruth in that book—she's one of my favorite characters. She really does want to rise above her background and poverty, and make something more of her life than her sisters ever accomplished, and she respects, even grows to love, Foster Williams, for giving her this chance. And yet she has no role model—no script for how she should talk or act, and she keeps blowing it at every turn.[12]

To the extent that April Ruth grows from being almost a spoiled pet of the much older Foster into a young woman of spirit determined to be a true partner in the relationship, she resembles Naylor's development throughout her first marriage, during which time she "left her doormat status behind" and weathered the storm, becoming stronger in the process, as Naylor describes in an interview with Kay Bonetti.[13] Through her experiences with her first husband, Naylor learned the healing and strengthening power of being able to admit to vulnerability, something Foster and April Ruth both learn. Naylor is proud to say that critically acclaimed author Ann Tyler read this book and liked it, saying, "These are such good people."[14]

But the origins of the characters in *Unexpected Pleasures* are not explicitly inherent in Naylor's life. She says the impetus for the novel came one night when her husband left their bed for a time. When he returned, she was very aware of her body and of the way she stretched and rolled, then curled herself up to make room for him beside her once more. She remembers thinking, "I'm going to put that in a book." At first she thought she would have a child sleeping with a sibling. If two children were sharing a bed, she thought, they might logically be from a blue collar family, so she decided they would be on a sofa bed in a trailer. And then, suddenly, she seemed to hear her character saying, "Thomasine, put that down. I'm gonna hit ya!" She had no idea where that line would appear in the story, but these two events provided the genesis of the book.[15]

Both the dialogue and Naylor's attention to detail are important strengths of this book. Foster eats white "Wonderbread" because it is consistent with his lifestyle; he shops for himself, buying whatever is cheapest wherever he can find a convenience store. When April Ruth moves in with Foster and tries her hand at cooking, she discovers "Cool Whip." Naylor says this product, because it is "cheap and easy," tells the reader a good deal about how April Ruth approaches life.

When Naylor envisioned Foster, she knew he had to be husky and strong; she turned to her "Occupations" file to find a job for him that would reflect his personality. She found a two-inch thick folder on bridge workers that she had collected over a 12-year period and decided this would be a perfect match for Foster, reflecting both his physique and his reserved nature. She had some difficulty finding a role model for Foster at first. She would call Bethlehem Steel or American Steel and Wire and ask to speak with someone who could tell her about building the second Chesapeake Bay bridge, but invariably she would be connected with an upper level administrator—in a suit and tie—instead of someone who actually spent his days high above the water attaching steel beams together. Beginning to despair, she received a phone call from a retired ironworker who said, "I built that bridge. What do you want to know?" He had even experienced the kind of fall that would eventually send Foster to the hospital. Naylor spent a good deal of time on the telephone with him. She also visited him in order to see the training films he now showed to new workers needing to learn how to walk on a nine-inch beam and even sent him relevant manuscript pages because she wanted to be exact about the nuances of Foster's daily life:

> I'd read that they ate their lunch on this barge, but then how did they get up to the bridge? Is there a lift? Is there a ladder? Is the ladder on the barge? Every single thing you have to know for sure. . . . For instance, you don't just say, "Give me that number two wrench." They may have a special name for it. . . . And he would give me the names so that it would ring true.

Naylor is particularly proud of the fact that this retired ironworker came to a book-signing party for *Unexpected Pleasures* and praised her, which she says means more to her than any review. He told her that when he had first talked with her, he had thought she would never be able to write the book. But at the party he said, "You did it! There's not one false note!"[16] His words gave Naylor a confidence about herself as a writer that she treasures, and this novel is still the one of which she is the most fond.

6. On Writing for Children and Adults— or Naylor Diversified: Picture Books, the "Witch" Books, Books for Elementary and Adult Readers

Although Naylor is a prolific and successful writer for young adults, she would prefer not to be categorized as a young adult author. She takes pride in the fact that critics admire her versatility, her ability to write for very young children, elementary readers, and adults as well as for adolescents. What motivates this shift from one audience to another? There are two notions, Naylor says. First of all, she does not want to be bored and fears that limiting herself to just one audience would cause her to lose interest in those readers. Second, she does not want the critics to stereotype her; she wants to keep them guessing about what she will do next.[1] And she likes to give herself a break between similar books so her words will be fresh and original.

Naylor admits, however, that she finds writing for adults and young children more difficult than writing for adolescents and preadolescents. Writing for adults is "harder in that it's longer, and for me at least, it's much more complex. . . . there are many more subplots. I delve deeper into personalities, into motivation; the threads get much more tangled."[2] But she finds writing picture books even more challenging, saying, "The hardest thing for me to write is a picture book because it is much more like poetry."[3] She feels that all writing takes "precision and care" and notes that it is the protagonist who shapes a story. For example, Naylor notes that if she has an 11-year-old as the protagonist and adultery surfaces in the plot, clearly the protagonist is not the participant. Readers will, however, experience the situation through the eyes of that 11-year-old and will know clearly how it affects the child who has to live with all the uncertainties of such an event.[4]

The "precision and care" for which Naylor is noted in her young adult novels is very much in evidence in her work for other audiences. She explores many of the same themes and demonstrates her personal value system in the range of her work. Naylor's commitment to hard work—evidenced in the amount of time she spends in research and the care she takes to find just the right detail of place and environment—is a factor in many of her titles. Despite her diligence she claims, "I don't like research! I want to rush headlong into the story."[5] She often presents characters, both the younger protagonists and the adults in their lives, engaged in interesting occupations.

Naylor views herself as a religious person, although she says she has no particular creed. As a result of her own beliefs and the way in which she came to question her parents' religious convictions, she often shows characters wrestling with theological issues in her books. Because she struggled to determine a sense of self that was somewhat different from the identity that first her parents, and then her first husband, held for her, the theme of creating an independent personality flows throughout her work. Coming to know and accept oneself can require creative problem solving, another dominant theme, as is the need to face fear head-on, both the kind of fear that comes from within, and the kind that arises as an individual confronts the external world. Furthermore, as has been noted, Naylor has a tendency to ascribe the desire to be a "maker," an artisan, and a "doer" to her young adult characters. This hunger is one that many of her protagonists of all ages share with their author!

The Importance of Hard Work

Jean Karl, who has served as one of Naylor's editors for over 25 years, comments on Naylor's development as a writer:

> Over the years I think her abilities as a writer have improved in that she has learned to delve deeper into her subject matter in some of her books. She has also developed a stronger style, while at the same time has learned to vary her approach in the books she writes. . . . She is *always* glad to have comments and to rework what she has done. . . . I enjoy working with Phyllis. She is always responsive and is a responsible writer, one who cares about her work and wants it to be the best she can make it. An author of that sort is always good to edit.[6]

Naylor takes her craft very seriously. *Ice,* which earned a starred review in *School Library Journal,*[7] went through 17 drafts. At times Naylor was convinced she would never see the end of this book; she even suggested giving it up. But Karl believed that the book would come together, and so Naylor kept working and eventually was able to say, "I did what I wanted to do." Currently she is at work on an adult novel and already knows she will have to do a good deal of revision. After listening to a mystery by Sue Grafton on tape, Naylor evaluated her own craft in light of what she perceives as Grafton's skill in describing exactly what her characters are wearing or what their mannerisms are when performing even a routine action like picking a newspaper off the floor. She thought, "Aah! This can get so tedious . . . but it does really help." She decided "This is really important. I'm going to have to go back over this adult novel I've written and *see* the whole thing, not just jump from one conversation to the next." Naylor told interviewer Kay Bonetti that she's not a visual person, so

> I'm trying to force myself when I go on my two mile walk to think about what I'm seeing, to remember it, to liken it to something else. Buds on a box elder look like those bristles on an old toothbrush, or something like that. And I'm trying to improve my visual sense of things.[8]

Naylor's personal work ethic is one that many of her characters either have to learn or already demonstrate. It demands that she write every day, that she keep track of articles that grab her attention, that she call experts in a given field to ensure accuracy, and that she constantly assess her strengths and weaknesses. *Eddie Incorporated* (1980) and *Josie's Troubles* (1992) are both about young people in elementary school who have to find ways to make enough money to do something they want or need to do. When Josie and a friend accidentally break the leg off a piano stool, they have to pay for the repairs, and the story follows their efforts to generate the money. Their first efforts—as pet sitters— fail: They kill the fish for which they are responsible, and a dog they are walking breaks loose and runs away. But they do not give up, and eventually they not only repay the money spent to fix the stool, they develop a deep-seated satisfaction from the work itself.

In the six "Witch" books, the main character, Lynn, and her friend Mouse, work in the bookstore owned by Mouse's father. They take pride, as Alice does when she works on Saturday's in her father's music store, in dusting and caring for the books and in organizing the shelves, unpacking deliveries, and cleaning the glass fronts of the rare books cases (*Witch Weed*, 69). Lynn frequently baby-sits her younger brother, and she takes this responsibility very seriously as well. Her mother routinely leaves her notes that tell her to "make beds, run carpet sweeper over downstairs rugs, do lunch dishes, keep an eye on Stevie" (*Witch's Sister*, 11).

In the biographical *Maudie in the Middle* (1988), written with her mother about her mother's childhood in the Midwest, Naylor illustrates the importance of having a family in which each member pulls his or her own weight. The preadolescent boys in *Wrestle the Mountain* (1971), *To Walk the Sky Path* (1973), and *Shiloh* (1991) contribute to their families' incomes and shoulder, usually cheerfully, their share of the household chores. In the adult novel *Revelations* (1979), Jake, a middle-school boy whose parents have died, comes to live with his Aunt Mary in a rural Maryland town and takes a job with a traveling carnival. In spite of the gritty reality of carnival life, Jake values his job as a way to achieve a measure of independence. He takes pride in doing it well because that makes him feel good about himself, just as Brad from *To Shake a Shadow*, Nick from *The Keeper*, or George, from *The Year of the Gopher*, do.

Throughout the body of her work, Naylor shows adult characters achieving self-respect in whatever career or job they have chosen, and she is careful to portray the details of their work experiences accurately. In the descriptions of Bernie, the preadolescent protagonist of the "Bessledorf" books, young readers gain insight into what it takes to run a hotel. Bernie's sister works in a parachute factory, and Bernie encounters a funeral parlor director in one of the series titles. In the Witch books, Lynn's father is a lawyer, and her mother is a writer, and Lynn reflects for the reader on the pros and cons of those professions. Eddie's father owns a produce store, and his older brother Roger clerks in a shoe store; at the dinner table, they discuss the ups and downs of their days. In the picture book *Meet Murdock* (1969), readers are introduced to Murdock, a building superintendent, and in *One of the Third Grade Thonkers* (1988; hereafter cited as *Thonkers*), Naylor provides a detailed look at what it is like to work on a towboat.

The story of *One of the Third Grade Thonkers* illustrates how clearly Naylor can create a vision of the future for her young readers. When Naylor's family moved to Joliet, Illinois, where the book takes place, Naylor started seventh grade. At that time, Joliet presented a sharp contrast to the sleepy, small town in southern Indiana where she had been living. She describes her delight with Joliet in vivid terms:

> When I entered Joliet it was a big ethnic town. My friends had last names like Seron and Perona and Heironimus. The high school was outstanding. It was a huge school, two thousand students, and they had the most marvelous productions, operettas and madrigal groups, and the band was nationally famous: It was so vibrant and exciting. I loved that town!

Until the death of her sister in 1993, Naylor visited Joliet periodically. Arriving in the city by train one time, her favorite form of long-distance travel, Naylor was struck by the ugliness and dirtiness of its industrial section. She decided to write a story about a child growing up in such a place. As she began to shape the story, her first thoughts were about how to create a specific sense of place:

> If he's in Joliet, what is specific to Joliet? . . . It's the river running through it and the drawbridges. Every time you want to go east or west to make a train or catch a bus, you have to see if the bridges are up or down and which way the boat's going and try to beat it. And I thought, "That would be interesting. Not everybody lives in a town like that."

Thinking about the river made Naylor recall that her sister's husband, while in college, had worked on a towboat one summer, and she decided to make the father of one of her characters a towboat man. But she needed information, details about that lifestyle, in order to create the feeling of reality and tension she knew families felt when the river was high, and the towboats were in danger. Planning a trip to Joliet for a family reunion, she wrote to the public librarian. "I didn't even know her name—it was really a case of chutzpah!" She said she wanted to do such a book and asked for help gathering information from the vertical files.

When Naylor arrived in town, she found that the librarian had gone above and beyond the call of duty. She had found a lot of articles, had copied them and taped them together, and had even set up a conference for Naylor with six retired towboat operators. "So, I sat and listened to them talk. It was so interesting just to hear them; they sort of forgot I was there. They started swapping these wild stories, and I was writing as fast as I could." Naylor tells this story to illustrate both her eagerness to make sure she "gets things right" when writing about occupations and to demonstrate how much she appreciates the kindness of others who "help her along the way" as she conducts the research that will allow her readers get inside the heads and hearts of her characters.

On Confronting Fear and
the Nature of Bravery

Naylor included some of those stories in her book, which is dedicated to the towboat men of Joliet. Jimmy, one of the two main characters, is the son of Bart Novak, who runs a towboat that pushes barges on the Mississippi. Toward the end of the book, Jimmy is terrified when he learns that there has been an accident on the river. Either something has happened with the steering, or the current caused the accident, but in either event, the tow of barges has broken apart—and that means the cables have snapped. Jimmy's dad was on the lead barge, helping to navigate a bend in the river, and now the barge is missing. Jimmy's fear stems from his knowledge of towboat life:

> He knew that a steel cable, snapping, could whip around and cut a person in two, like a hatchet. He knew that's how a man named James Henshaw had died. He knew that's how Clyde Perkins lost a leg. When barges sideswiped each other or a bank, when they turned or jackknifed on a river, you didn't want to be anywhere near a snapping cable. . . .
>
> It seemed to him now, as he sat alone on the back steps, that the river had become an enemy with a hundred tricks for catching a man and his boat.
>
> Fog, for one thing. "Surface fog," his father called it, because it was worse right there above the water, right where the pilot needed to see. Currents were another. When the river was high, as the Mississippi was now, the currents were unpredictable. There was the suction, too, created by two boats passing each other, which could pull a boat into another one. And of course there were the shadows that might not be shadows at all. When you walked the length of a tow, from one barge to another, one misstep could put you in the water. (*Thonkers*, 109–10)

Jimmy's experience in waiting for word of his father, which comes within a few hours and is good news, makes him reevaluate his perceptions of his cousin, David. David has been living with Jimmy for several weeks because his mother, Jimmy's aunt, has had a serious heart problem and has been in intensive care for some time after a complicated operation. Like Jimmy, David is in third grade—although he is a year younger—and is scared of almost everything; he even wets the bed sometimes at night. David is a picky eater, and he wears clothes that match, all of which contributes to Jimmy's belief that David is a sissy. Jimmy, on the other hand, is a "Thonker," one of a group of boys who have formed a club because they have been brave in the face of physical pain. Jimmy had an operation on his knee, and his friend Sam had his arm in a cast, and Peter had been in a car accident. The three boys are the envy of their classmates; they have special tee shirts, they ride their bikes in formation, and they attempt daredevil acts to further their status as "Thonkers: Rough, Tough, and Terrible" (*Thonkers*, 5).

David, of course, wants to be a Thonker, but given the fact that he cries when he hurts his mouth eating a Frito, there does not seem to be any hope for him, especially when Jimmy and friends plan a reckless prank. They are going to "ride" a railroad bridge to prove their bravery. Usually, counterweights are in the down position on a railroad bridge, holding it up in the air so that boats can travel freely underneath. But when a train is coming, the counterweights move up, and the roadbed, with tracks on it, comes down and lines up with tracks on either side of the river. The Thonkers plan to wait for a train to roll toward the bridge, climb onto the platform the moment the train passes by, and ride that platform as it is raised back into the air, jumping down before the bridge is back in place.

The three boys actually carry out their scheme, but Jimmy does not feel brave afterward. As the boys ride their bikes back home, rehearsing what they will tell their friends at school, Jimmy starts to feel sick inside: "It *had* been dangerous, and Jimmy knew it. Dark and dangerous and just plain dumb. When they jumped, Jimmy had been too high, and they hadn't counted on the bounce or the roll. There were a lot of things they hadn't counted on" (*Thonkers*, 104).

David is waiting for Jimmy when they boys return to their club-house—Jimmy's garage—with the news of the towboat accident. Jimmy sends the other boys home and begins some intense soul-searching while waiting for morning and news of his father. He finally realizes the measure of David's courage, thinking that, whereas he himself has to wait only a few hours, David

> had gone days without knowing whether his mom would be all right. First the heart operation, then the hours that Aunt Lois had spent in the recovery room, then the days she had spent in intensive care. . . . He wondered if he himself would have been brave enough to get on a plane alone and fly to another city, not knowing what was happening with his mother back home. How did David stand it? It must have been the most difficult thing he had ever done. (*Thonkers*, 123)

Jimmy recognizes the difference between being brave—"doing something dangerous and scary because somebody *has* to do it" (*Thonkers*, 126), like his dad on the barge, or like David—and simply being stupid. As a result of this insight, Jimmy invites David into the Thonkers' clubhouse and convinces the other boys to make David a member of the Thonkers as well.

Naylor is sad that *One of the Third Grade Thonkers* never received the recognition she feels it deserves. She likes the subject—the nature of bravery, which is a theme she explores in many of her titles, including a very explicit treatment of it in *The Fear Place* (1994). Like Ellen from *Night Cry* (1984), 12-year-old Doug has to confront his worst fears in an emergency situation. Doug's family is camping in the Rocky Mountains, but the death of Doug's uncle calls his parents away. They are certain that Doug and his older brother Gordon can survive on their own for a day or two, with a park ranger to check on them, but the parents are not aware of the depth of the antagonism the two brothers feel for each other. Gordon has always teased Doug—almost to the point of tears—about his fear of heights. Once their parents have left the campsite, not only does the teasing begin in earnest, but the boys begin squabbling over food and chores. Naylor describes with devastating accuracy the anger the younger Doug feels when Gordon refuses to take his turn dealing with the garbage.

He had known it was going to be this way after the folks left. Gordon would get out of doing everything. Doug didn't know if his stomach hurt because he was hungry or because he was angry. White-hot fire stabbed at his temples. His jaw felt like a nutcracker.... Anger was a ball of heat in his throat. As he passed Gordon on the ground, he swung the bag [of garbage] sideways, just to bump him a bit. The banana peels, bacon wrapping, and grapefruit rinds rained down on Gordon's chest, dropping in smelly clumps on his lap. (*The Fear Place*, 38)

The two boys get into a knock-down-drag-out fight, and Gordon takes off, leaving Doug alone at the campsite.

A cougar enters into the picture. As Doug is hiking on his own, he sees a flash of tawny color, a sleek body and quivering tail, ahead of him on the trail. Doug panics, recalling every story he knows about wildcats attacking people in the wilderness, but strangely, this cougar seems content to follow a few paces behind him. Doug decides to see if he can get the cougar to show itself again and hopes that Gordon will return to camp to see Doug and the cat in action. Gordon does not return, but the cougar does, and after several encounters with it, the cougar, now called "Charlie," gets so close to the boy that Doug can feel its breath on his ankles. Over a period of several days, Doug and the cat develop a relationship of sorts, one that Doug is careful not to jeopardize by trying to touch it, for instance.

Doug overcomes his fear of Charlie, but he learns the meaning of a new kind of apprehension when Gordon continues to be absent from camp. Doug realizes that Gordon has not taken enough supplies—not enough food or water—to support him for the time he has been gone. On top of all this, his parents have failed to reappear. The morning after Doug has expected his parents, he knows he will have to go in search of Gordon. In doing so, he will have to climb to "the fear place," a ridge that evokes all of Doug's anxiety about heights; he will have to search an area that he has refused to walk for several years. Surprisingly, Charlie shows him how to negotiate the ledge, and Doug makes it to the other side, where he finds Gordon, leg broken, feverish, moving in and out of consciousness. It is up to Doug to get his brother back down the mountain. Putting a splint on the badly damaged ankle, he sets out with Gordon, piggyback style, and begins following Charlie back down the mountain, telling Gordon the story of the cat to keep their minds off the danger they are in. During the descent, the boys manage to work out some of their differences,

The Upper Narrows, Long's Peak. Naylor's son Mike and friends. Photo taken by older son, Jeff. It was their climb to the summit that inspired *The Fear Place*.

and they resolve, if they survive, to be better brothers, better friends.

Naylor, who has a fear of heights, started writing *The Fear Place* on the day her sons were climbing Long's Peak. She says, "It was one of the worst days of my life. I wouldn't have tried to stop them for anything because it's something they really wanted to do, and they're both capable and responsible. But I thought, 'The only way I can get through this is to think it into a book, to get it out and onto paper. . . .' When it's on paper, you are a god, and you're deciding whether or not they will come through okay. Just getting my mind on something else that day was my salvation." Her sons were young men at this time; one was married, but still Naylor worried about them. Today she cannot pick up the book, cannot read the description of Doug going over just the sort of ledge her sons had to navigate, because "it's just too frightening."

On the Importance of Being a Creative Problem Solver

Naylor's ability to use her anxiety to produce a good book demonstrates the creative problem-solving ability with which she often endows her characters. In *King of the Playground* (1991), a picture book, Kevin's problem is Sammy. Kevin loves going to the playground, but Sammy, who calls himself "King of the Playground," terrorizes Kevin, threatening to do awful things to him if he tries to use "Sammy's" swings or slide or monkey bars. Kevin tells his father, "Sammy says if I climb the monkey bars, he'll come over to our house and nail all the doors and windows shut and we'll be trapped forever" (*King*). Kevin's father helps him think the situation through; they decide that while Sammy is nailing one door shut, they could just sneak out the other. The next day, Kevin dons his Spiderman tee shirt, his Batman underwear, and, feeling "only a little bit brave and a little bit lucky" (*King*), sets off to confront his adversary, who presents a new challenge each day. Sammy is in the sandbox, playing alone, having scared away all the other children.

Kevin puts first one foot and then the other into the sand, and Sammy starts threatening him, saying he will put Kevin in a cage with bears. Kevin calmly begins to play in the sandbox, replying that he will just teach the bears tricks. Their battle of language goes on until Kevin says if Sammy comes after him, he will drive away in a truck. Sammy bellows that he will get a tank and chase the truck into the ocean. Kevin challenges him to try it, and he starts building a tunnel for his truck. Sammy, not believing his eyes and ears, starts digging a tunnel from his side of the sandbox. Then Kevin changes the game again, bragging that he will build the biggest fort in the world.

> "Ha!" said Sammy. "It's got to have towers."
> "It will," Kevin said.
> "It's got to have a drawbridge," said Sammy.
> "It will," Kevin said.
> "It's got to have a ditch all around," said Sammy.
> "It will," Kevin said. "Help me build it."
> "No," Sammy told him. But he did. (*King*)

And Kevin's problem has been solved.

In this picture book, Naylor explores the idea that the person who acts in an unsociable, disagreeable, and even threatening or harmful manner can be challenged with humor and affection that arise from understanding the other person's loneliness. This is a theme she develops in more depth in many of her titles. Ellen, from *Night Cry*, for instance, puzzles over why Gerald went wrong given what she perceived as his hard-working nature. She tries to befriend him—with food and conversation—until she ascertains that he is a kidnapper. Craig, from *The Dark of the Tunnel*, is able to connect with Cougar, feared by other townspeople, because he views the wild man as an artist and assumes, therefore, that they share a similar way of looking at the world. Alice deals with the bully Denise by using a middle-school version of Kevin's strategy; she asks to be Denise's partner for an English project and writes about Denise's positive qualities in her essay. Denise is used to being feared, not appreciated, and, having been caught off guard by Alice's response, she shows her softer side to Alice.

In the Witch series, Naylor explores this theme most fully. She wrote six of these books, all of which deal with the efforts of Lynn, a sixth grader, and her friend Mouse, to deal with the evil Mrs. Tuggle, a neighbor who lives in a terrifying house and who has dark, magical powers. She uses her magic, in different books, to control various members of Lynn's family and wants desperately to lure Lynn and Mouse into her clutches. *Witch's Sister* (1975), *Witch Water* (1977), and *The Witch Herself* (1978) are the first Witch trilogy. In the first book, Lynn and Mouse operate on their own, with little adult help, because they know adults want facts, not conjecture, and they have no proof that Mrs. Tuggle has been attempting to make Lynn's sister, Judith, a part of her coven. In the second book, Mrs. Tuggle seems to have a great deal of influence over Lynn's mother, and Lynn feels how easy it would be to give in to her fear, to do whatever Mrs. Tuggle asks of her—and in return, to obtain power over people and things. She recognizes that Mrs. Tuggle represents an evil that is present within herself, and probably within everyone—an evil that drives individuals into power-hungry and inhumane ways of acting. She perceives that "this is the most dangerous thing of all. . . . The attraction was there, whether she liked it or not" (*Witch Water*, 34). During the events of *The Witch Herself*, Lynn confronts her darker side more explicitly, telling Mouse,

> "Dorella is the evilness in me, just as there is evilness in everybody! People have always been a mixture of good and bad, you know that. Only Mrs. Tuggle has a way of communicating with this evilness. ∴. . She wants to make Dorella in me stronger, too, but she won't do it Mouse! I won't let it happen! As long as I know, as long as I can fight, Dorella doesn't stand a chance."
> (*The Witch Herself*, 73)

Because her mother has been acting so oddly, Lynn confides her dread of Mrs. Tuggle and of witchcraft to her father; he helps her recognize that even if Mrs. Tuggle represents some darker power, Lynn has to accept responsibility for herself and her actions; if she teases her brother and makes him cry, she cannot blame witchcraft. As the old woman seemingly dies, Lynn knows that she has not seen the death of "her own demon" (*The Witch Herself*, 162). She will have to take control of her own life.

Ten years after the publication of *The Witch Herself*, a second publisher approached Naylor about doing a series. Naylor wrote *The Witch's Eye* in 1990, *Witch Weed* in 1991, and *The Witch Returns* in 1992 for Delacorte Press. Mouse is almost sucked into Mrs. Tuggle's world in the first of the new trilogy, other young girls in the town are threatened in the second, and Lynn almost succumbs in the third. Evidence of Mrs. Tuggle's otherworldliness mounts to the point that the adults in Lynn's life can no longer ignore Lynn's ideas. After Lynn sets a huge fire in *Witch Weed* as a last-ditch measure to destroy the vegetation that is luring so many young girls into Mrs. Tuggle's circle, an act so out of character and so inexplicable, Lynn's father sends her to a psychiatrist. Realizing that he is dealing with a phenomenon outside his realm of expertise, the doctor enlists the aid of both Lynn's parents and Mouse's father. Mr. Beasely owns a rare manuscript of spells and potions. A new and even scarier old woman, Mrs. Gullone, who shows up in Mrs. Tuggle's house claiming to be her sister, seems determined to get her hands on it.

But it is Lynn who figures out how to get rid of the witch once and for all. In a final showdown, Lynn asks that everyone who believes in the witch join hands to create a "circle of good will" that will keep the evilness *in* and allow them to squeeze it into nothingness.

> If Mrs. Gullone could summon the potential for evil inside others, then perhaps Lynn could summon up something from long ago in Mrs. Gullone—something that had once been good and innocent, before the witchcraft began. (*The Witch Returns*, 174)

Lynn calls out the name of the child Mrs. Tuggle/Gullone had once been.

> Instantly, a black cloud covered the moon, darkening the whole backyard. The wind blew and whistled in their ears, and Lynn bent her head against the onslaught. But still the circle

remained, still their hands held fast, and the moon came out again. (*The Witch Returns*, 176)

The witch disappears, almost as if she has melted. All that is left is a heap of clothes and a kitten, "such a *new* little thing" (*The Witch Returns*, 177), which Lynn explains by saying, "What was left was the small seed of goodness that had once, long ago, been a young girl named Ellie Martin, and wanting to live after being a prisoner for so long, the goodness had sprung to life as a kitten" (*The Witch Returns*, 178). Throughout the plots of six novels Lynn and Mouse have fought to find a way to confront and defeat the witch. It is only when they stop using her own methods and turn the tables on her, assuming that there is a "seed of goodness" buried deep inside, that they are finally able to rid their world of the witch.

The Witch books are scary books, in part because Naylor is so adept at using weather imagery to create an atmosphere of tension and fear, and in part because the reader is never really certain, until close to the end of the series, whether or not Mrs. Tuggle is truly a witch. Tuggle's ability to call out the demons inside everyone she encounters is the truly frightening thing about her. Readers have to see themselves in Lynn as she struggles to overcome those parts of herself that are less honorable, less humane.

In Naylor's Newbery winner, *Shiloh* (1991), there is no doubt about the humanness of Judd Travers—but there is also no doubt that he is a truly vile man. Marty Preston, a young boy of 11, has to find a way to win Judd's respect in order to go on with his life. Like Lynn, Marty uses some clever thinking to even the odds when he goes up against Judd.

Shiloh is a hound dog that has been ill treated by Travers and has run away. Marty finds the dog and takes him home, but his father insists that the boy return the hound to its rightful owner. Marty's dad is a legalistic thinker and, as a poor man, recognizes the difficulties involved in making a neighbor angry. In Mr. Preston's eyes, Marty has no choice, even though Judd is known to cheat shopkeepers out of their change, to spit tobacco as close as he can to those he does not like, to shoot deer out of season, and to beat his dogs. Marty, on the other hand, believes that Judd's claim to the dog is negated by his lack of care and concern for the animal, and he feels it is his duty to take care of it. Nevertheless, Marty does what his dad tells him and hands a trembling, shaking, dog over to Judd.

When the dog runs away again and shows up at Marty's house, Marty determines to hide and care for it without his parents' knowledge. He eats only half of his meals, saving the rest for the dog. He collects cans for the recycling fee and scrounges scraps from the store for the dog. He lies about what he is doing so that he can spend time with Shiloh, but discovers that one subterfuge creates another: "Funny how one lie leads to another and before you know it, your whole life can be a lie" (*Shiloh*, 60).

Marty also finds himself getting sassy, and he confronts Judd in the middle of the book, foreshadowing the climax. Judd is looking for his dog and stops his truck to ask Marty if he has seen him.

> "You got to treat a dog good if you want him to stick around," I say, bold as brass. . . .
>
> "I figure a dog's the same as a kid. You don't treat a kid right, he'll run off the first chance he gets."
>
> Judd laughs. "Well, if that was true, I would have run when I was four. Far back as I remember Pa took a belt to me—big old welts on my back so raw I could hardly pull my shirt on. I stuck around. Didn't have anyplace else to go. I turned out, didn't I?"
>
> "Turned out how?" The boldness in my chest is growing, taking all the air.
>
> Now Judd sounds mad. "You tryin' to be smart with me, boy?"
>
> "No. Just asking how you turned out, somebody who was beat since he was four. I feel sorry is what I feel." . . .
>
> "Well, don't you go wasting your time feeling sorry for me. . . . Sorry is something I can do without." (*Shiloh*, 63–64)

Marty's mom follows him one night and learns he has been caring for Shiloh. She is adamant; he will have to tell his father in the morning. That night, however, a neighbor dog, a huge German shepherd, attacks Shiloh, and Marty's dad finds out before Marty is able to come clean. Shiloh is badly injured in the fight, and Marty feels responsible. Had he not shut Shiloh up in a pen, Shiloh might have been able to run away. But he still feels he can do better by the dog than Judd can. The whole family joins in the conspiracy of silence around Shiloh. After Marty and his dad take Shiloh to the doctor (there is no vet), the father agrees to let Marty keep the dog in the house until its injuries have healed. At that time he will have to figure out a way to deal with Travers on his own.

Marty is on his way to talk to Judd when he catches him shooting a deer out of season. His first response is to barter, offering not to tell the game warden what he has witnessed in exchange for the dog. Judd offers a deal. If Marty will stay silent and work for him for 20 hours, at two dollars an hour, he can have the dog. Marty agrees, but he does not feel comfortable with this idea, however, thinking, "I began to see I'm no better than Judd Travers—willing to look the other way to get something I want. But the something is Shiloh. . . I'm thinkin' straight enough as I help drag that doe to Judd's to know that by lettin' him get away with this, I'm putting other deer in danger" (*Shiloh*, 125).

Marty works at back-breaking tasks for two weeks, doing chores that are not safe for an 11-year-old, like splitting wood with a sledge hammer. Judd is a difficult master, finding fault with almost everything Marty does, and making him redo. Marty knows that by the time he has earned the $40 he needs to buy Shiloh, all trace of the shooting of the doe will have vanished, so he is in suspense wondering if Judd will actually uphold his end of the bargain. But Marty's determination to do his work and not allow Judd's taunts to rile him, pay off. When Judd does or says something mean, Marty gives a kindness back. For instance, one day Judd pretends to be asleep. Marty figures Judd wants him to go home—and then he will say there is no proof that Marty kept his end of the bargain. So Marty finds another chore. He weeds the garden for an extra hour. When Judd pretends to awaken, Marty starts for home. Judd yells that he will not pay a cent extra for overtime. Marty says he understands and reflects that "[I] never saw a look on a man's face like I see on his. Pure puzzlement is what it is" (*Shiloh*, 140). Marty makes an effort to say nice things to Judd, complimenting him on his other dogs, asking him how he got interested in hunting, and by the time his 40 hours of work detail are over, Judd gives the boy a collar for the dog. Marty muses that "I don't know how we done it, but somehow we learned to get along" (*Shiloh*, 144).

By the end of the novel, Marty still is not clear about the morality of everything he has done. He figures that he has learned a lot, however, through his efforts to make Shiloh his own. He realizes that nothing is as simple as it seems and knows he should feel good about saving Shiloh and about the lessons he has learned from his experiences.

Shiloh was Naylor's creative solution to her own real-life encounter with a mistreated dog. Naylor and her husband, Rex, were visiting friends in West Virginia. One morning they took a walk along a wide creek in the little community called Shiloh. Naylor realized something was following them, and it turned out to be a dog, a beagle mixed with lots of other breeds. "It was the saddest looking dog I had ever seen—skinny, ill-kept, hungry, and obviously mistreated. Its tail was wagging hopefully, but every time I put out my hand to touch it, the dog trembled and shook and crawled away on its belly as though I were about to do it bodily harm."[9] The dog did, however, respond to a whistle, and it followed the Naylors all the way back to their friends' home. All day the dog sat outside, in driving rain, head on its paws, looking at the house. Naylor was so upset about this dog, in spite of her friends' explanation that *many* unwanted animals are turned loose to fend for themselves in the woods, that Rex and the other man took the dog back over the bridge and tried to find its home. They were unsuccessful, so they let it out beside a house with a bike in front of it and took off. The dog followed—but could not catch up.

Throughout the entire afternoon's drive back home to Maryland, Naylor says she "talked tearfully of nothing but the dog."[10] Finally her husband challenged her, saying, "Well, Phyllis, are you going to have a nervous breakdown, or are you going to do something about it?"[11] She decided to do something— and created Marty Preston as a way to save that dog. The real-life

Phyllis Naylor and husband Rex Naylor with the dog now named Clover, whom they met in Shiloh, West Virginia, and who is called Shiloh in the Newbery-winning book, *Shiloh*.

The bridge leading to Judd Travers's trailer home in Shiloh, West Virginia (the setting for *Shiloh*).

"Shiloh" found a happy home just like Marty's Shiloh does. The Naylors' friends were out walking a week or so after the Naylor visit. The dog showed up again, and this time they found they could not refuse its affections. They fed it, took it to the vet, cleaned it up, bought it a collar, and named it "Clover." They now describe Clover as "the happiest dog in West Virginia."[12]

On the Importance of Community

In the Witch books, Lynn, Mouse, and the adults all work *together* to deal with their problem. Frequently Naylor emphasizes the importance of community in dealing with adversity. In *An Amish Family* (1974), Naylor demonstrates that it is the sense of community and communal responsibility—for building homes, for tilling fields, for raising the young in the faith—that has allowed the Amish to maintain their way of life over the years. In *To Walk the Sky Path* (1973; hereafter cited as *To Walk*), Billie, a young Seminole who is the first of his family to attend the public elementary school, constantly reflects on the importance of community to the Seminole—a value he does not always see honored among his classmates. Billie does not understand the competitiveness of white society, wondering "What kind of pride did white people have that they had to top somebody else to be important?" (*To Walk*, 24). After a hurricane wipes out Billie's village, Billie and his brother Charlie help with each step of the rebuilding process. It is accepted and expected that everyone pitch in to help everyone else; "What kind of man would not go where he was needed?" (*To Walk*, 87). As Grandfather says, "The true Indian is a man who remembers the ways of his forefathers, even in the white man's world, and who does not step on his brother to get more for himself" (*To Walk*, 137).

One of Naylor's most significant demonstrations of her belief in the power of community to overcome overwhelming odds occurs in *Wrestle the Mountain* (1971). Jed and his family live in an impoverished coal town deep in the mountains of West Virginia. A creek rises, flooding out much of the area, including Jed's aunt's home. Without being called, neighbors appear during the flood to rescue Aunt Ella and her husband, who has just recently lost his leg in a mining accident. When the flood recedes, they come again with buckets and mops and a determination to set things to rights. They also bring casseroles, preserves, and handmade items to replace the furniture and belongings Aunt Ella has lost to the waters of the flood. Ella realizes she cannot possibly use all these items, and so her creative juices start to flow. Perceiving that the community is rich in handcrafting talent, she decides they should work together to run a business to sell the things they make. They can open a store for tourists and also sell by mail. If the business takes off, the town will be less dependent on the fortunes of the mine.

> It was an exciting time. Nobody knew what would happen for sure, for it was their store and everyone took a part in fixing it up. Women came down to plant flowers in the strip of dirt between the store and dirt road. Uncle Caully stood on one leg, supported by his crutches and painted the inside walls white. Sedge Miles put shutters on the four front windows, and painted them red, and someone decided that the front door should be yellow and painted it one night when no one else was around. Some of the men got together and built display tables from rough lumber, and the women washed the windows and scrubbed the floor. It was, when it was finished, the nicest look-ing place in Tin Creek—the only nice place, in fact, and folks began to talk about fixing up other things, too. (*Wrestle the Mountain*, 183)

Community spirit keeps alive one's hopes for a better future. Working together for the good of the community, individuals begin to realize their ability to create something different for themselves as well.

On Using Humor

In her own life Naylor has found that humor is a valuable weapon for getting through difficult times. In many of her works for young adult readers, Naylor shows characters such as Alice, Beth from *Send No Blessings,* or Nick from *The Keeper* using humor in just this way. Theirs is simply a more sophisticated brand of the humor in some of Naylor's books for younger readers used to lighten the tone when dealing with issues such as the importance of community or the need for creative problem solving. One of the lessons that Andy learns in *Beetles, Lightly Toasted* (1987) is that he might be better off working *with* his cousin Jack than competing against him all the time. But before Andy can even begin to envision the possibilities of collaboration for creative projects, he spends a lot of time trying to beat Jack in an essay contest. The topic for the contest is "Conservation." Entrants are to describe their own innovative solution to an environmental problem, and Andy decides to write a paper about unusual sources of food. Most of the novel describes his efforts to test recipes for fried worms, toasted beetles, and ant larvae. While Andy watches, his friends and family unsuspectingly eat brownies made crunchy with beetles instead of nuts, egg salad extended with larvae, and fried chicken enhanced with deep-fried worms. For the reader, the humor derives, as it does for Andy, from being "in the know" while the other characters sink their teeth into food that sounds less than appetizing. In this passage, Andy has pressed his friend Sam, whose family owns a restaurant, into experimenting with the deep-frying of worms, whose intestinal tracts had been cleaned out on a diet of applesauce several days prior to the cooking. Just as they put their tidbits out to cool, along comes a health inspector.

> "Ummm," she said, sniffing the air. "Certainly smells good in here."
> Mr. Hollins smiled. "Special spices," he told her. "Five more than Colonel Sanders uses on *his* chicken."
> The inspector smiled too. "Garlic," she guessed, "ginger, pepper, paprika . . ." She reached out, and while Sam and Andy stared in horror, picked up one of the tiny pieces of fried worm and popped it in her mouth. . . .
> "Chewy," the inspector was saying. "Tastes like . . . I don't see how it can, but it does . . . tastes like applesauce. . . . The secret ingredient." And she went over to inspect the shelves. (*Beetles,* 97)

Meanwhile, Sam's younger sister, Denise, has also discovered their experiment. She gobbles up all the worms not eaten by the inspector and asks for more. Andy infers that the recipe must be okay and that he can include it in his essay.

The contest ends in a tie between Andy and his cousin. But when Andy wins the contest, the tables are turned. The newspaper photographer insists that Andy be shown actually eating his conservation food himself—and he realizes that the recipes are pretty good after all. The humor of exaggeration and dramatic irony carry the reader through this lighthearted book with a serious message.

On Dealing with Religious Issues

Part of Marty's dilemma about how to save Shiloh and deal with Judd arises from the fact that he is trying to save the dog on his own. Things become easier once his family knows he has been taking care of the dog. Another aspect of his problem stems from the fact that he has been raised in a Christian home and has difficulty reconciling various facets of his upbringing with Shiloh's situation. Grandma Preston has told him in no uncertain terms that liars go to hell. Marty would prefer to go to heaven. However, he also thinks that since only people—and not animals—are allowed in heaven, then he would not want to find himself in heaven looking down at Shiloh, sad and beaten. He knows that even when he does not tell outright lies about the dog, he still has prevaricated by what he has chosen not to tell. He prays to Jesus for guidance, asking, "Which you want me to do? Be one hundred percent honest and carry that dog back to Judd so that one of your creatures can be kicked and starved all over again, or keep him here and fatten him up to glorify your creation?" Marty concludes, "If Jesus is anything like the story cards from Sunday school make him out to be, he ain't the kind to want a thin, little beagle to be hurt" (*Shiloh*, p. 57).

Characters in other Naylor titles written for both younger children and adults deal explicitly with religious themes. They question what they have been taught and try to reconcile what they feel in their hearts with what their church says they should do. For instance, Maudie, from *Maudie in the Middle* (1988; hereafter cited as *Maudie*), is upset when her brother, Lester, spills her precious bottle of cologne. She has waited a long, long time for the cologne, which has just been delivered to the house by mail. She tries to recall what Sister Bliss would do.

> "Return evil with good," came to mind. She knew that however much she tried, she wasn't good enough yet to do something kind for Lester. To keep herself from doing something awful, in fact, was about as much as she could hope for. (*Maudie*, 53)

At another point in the book, Maudie decides she needs forgiveness for all her mistakes and character faults before she can get back on the right path and try to be a good person. Therefore, she is eager to take part in the foot-washing service at her church. She wants to have her own feet washed, symbolizing that she has been cleansed, and she wants to humble herself and wash another's feet, "just as Jesus did with his disciples" (*Maudie*, 85). But, exhausted, Maudie falls asleep during the lengthy service; her family, not knowing how much it means to her, lets her sleep. When she awakens, she is overcome with frustration and despair. In a touching scene, her mother, for once, focuses on the young girl and, at home, recreates the ceremony just for Maudie, who in turn lovingly washes her mother's feet and feels "[f]orgiveness at last" (*Maudie*, 90). In the end, Maudie knows that the struggle to be good will always be just that, a struggle. She understands that *real* goodness involves being kind to people even when they are not noticing her at all.

> The way to goodness, she decided, was like the path to the plum tree. Sometimes you went straight and sometimes you turned. Maudie might never be as blessed as Sister Bliss, but she might someday be as kind as Mother and Aunt Sylvie, and that was goodness enough. (*Maudie*, 161)

To Make a Wee Moon (1969) includes numerous scenes involving a preacher conducting tent revival meetings. Jean, the main character, is frustrated with her family's situation. Her parents have moved to the Midwest in the hope of making a new life for themselves as farmers, but in the meantime, they are living with Jean's grandmother and have no money; Jean is thus forced to wear the hand-me-downs of the only rich girl in the school. As is true for most elementary school children, Jean's greatest desire is to be a part of the group, to fit in. But outsiders, particularly those who dress and talk differently, are not welcomed. Jean is drawn to the revival meetings because she feels accepted there. She has many conversations about religion with Brother Bean, the preacher, and learns in the process that he has "done time." At first she thinks this is terrible, a violation of people's faith in him, but eventually she also realizes that true faith involves forgiving others—and oneself. As Brother Bean says, "The world is what we make it. Your house can be a palace or a prison, depends on how your mind sees it. The problem is not how to get what you don't have, but how to make do with what you have while you've got it" (*To Make a Wee Moon*, 184).

In addition to having served a jail sentence, it turns out that even as a minister, Brother Bean operates just inside the limits of the law—a fact that causes Jean more distress, although she eventually manages to forgive him even this. Bean travels with Murray Dawes, a carnival owner. The carnival sets up outside town, giving Brother Bean something against which to rant and rave in his sermons. People go to the carnival to see what is so awful about it, and Brother Bean and Murray split the take.

In *Revelations* (1979), a novel for adults, another Murray Dawes appears, only this time he is the evangelist. In this book Naylor juxtaposes a rigid fundamentalism with a livelier, more humanistic brand of faith preached by Murray—who now is in cahoots with another carnival manager. The novel centers on Mary, a spinster of 34, virtually the foundation of the church in which she grew up. Having taken care of her parents in their old age, she has never married and now spends her days at the church, acting as secretary. But when her wayward brother and his wife are killed in a plane crash, and their 14-year-old son Jake comes to live with her, she finds herself questioning not only her life as she has defined it, but her faith as well. Jake's willingness to challenge what he is told in Sunday school and his clear desire truly to understand theological issues make Mary insecure in her beliefs. And when Murray, a gifted orator dressed in white, sweeps her off her feet, Mary knows she will never be the same.

Mary's mother had taught her, as a child, to accept the taunts of the other children who laughed at her clothes and mannerisms as a "badge of distinction," to see her beliefs as a "source of strength," and to value their stares as "disguised manifestations of respect and envy" (*Revelations*, 41). But Mary has been feeling trapped in her life, in her faith. She lashes out in her insecurity when Jake starts to ask questions about what is in the Bible, drawing on her mother's answers in spite of the fact that she knows Jake is sincere in his desire to understand. Murray helps her, saying,

> "It's adolescence, Mary. It takes time to learn that there aren't scientific answers for everything. It's only after a person has experienced love and grief and jealousy and hate that he discovers there are facets of life which can't be measured by any other standards, can't be predicted or controlled or explained. And yet, as surely as he exists, he knows them to be present; he feels their hold on him. And he believes in something he has never seen or understood because he feels its power. Give him time, Mary. He'll come around." (*Revelations*, 207)

Later Murray emphasizes again that "Christianity's nothing if it's handed to you on somebody else's platter. It has to be a personal thing" (*Revelations*, 233). Even though Murray is run out of town by other members of Mary's church, in the end it is he who teaches her more about what it means to have a living faith—one that is based on love of others and forgiveness of shortcomings. He is contrasted with Milt Jennings, who proposes to Mary every New Year's Eve. Mary has thought about saying yes, so that Jake will have a father, but she just cannot bring herself to enter into a marriage of convenience rather than joy. Naylor exhibits her wit in describing how Mary thinks of Milt: "She wondered idly if perhaps God's plan was to keep Milt Jennings a bachelor all his life so there would be no more moon-faced children shouting Bible verses at the top of their lungs" (*Revelations*, 92). The one time Milt tries to kiss her, saying he is a "man with needs," he ruins the effect by spouting scripture at her, and Mary knows she will never marry him. Murray, however, teaches her to value her own body, to enjoy herself as a physical being. Mary comes to see that any religion that would deny the very real joy and communion of two people coming together in love is not in keeping with the image of the God in which she believes.

Mary and Naylor have a good deal in common. On the bookflap of *Revelations* Naylor remarks that she writes the revival scenes with such accuracy because she was "saved" so often herself as a young girl. Like Mary, Naylor came to break away from her parents' church. Like Mary, Naylor realized that neither the church nor any one person could make her feel whole and solve all her problems. In *Revelations* Naylor writes, "No matter how much you love someone, no matter how close you are, you still have to be on good terms with yourself because you still go through life alone. Your pain, your illnesses, your body still belong to you alone, and when you die, you go out of this world alone" (*Revelations*, 159). In a nonfiction title for Fortress, a Christian press, Naylor gives the same advice to young people in her book *How to Find Your Wonderful Someone* (1972).

Throughout her work, whether she is writing for young adults, children, or adults, Naylor draws from her personal experience and emphasizes the importance of developing a healthy sense of self in order to create healthy relationships with others, including God. Those characters who learn to work hard, confront their fears, use their creativity and other skills to solve the problems facing them, and who are willing to work within a community for the larger good are those who are best able to develop a robust inner self.

7. On Censorship, Connecting with Her Readers, and Being a Writer

Although Naylor describes herself as a religious person, has published numerous books with different Christian presses, and often writes about young people reflecting on religious issues, as in *Shiloh* and *A String of Chances*, she has often been the subject of censorship attacks from those who do not agree with her views. Naylor's presentation of religion, witchcraft, and young people questioning their parents, as well as her use of problematic language have resulted in numerous challenges to her books for both library and classroom settings.

On Dealing with Censorship

Books that have drawn fire most are those in the Witch series, *A String of Chances*, *The Year of the Gopher*, and *Shiloh*. Adult readers with strong religious views have disliked the witchcraft elements in Naylor's stories about Lynn and Mouse. Naylor says she does *not* believe in witchcraft. She wrote these books to have fun, "to write the scariest stories I could,"[1] while exploring the serious issue of how one confronts the darker elements of one's personality and also takes responsibility for living well. Young readers do not seem to have any difficulty with the inclusion of witchcraft. They simply enjoy reading scary books because doing so provides a safe way to experience aspects of life they otherwise would avoid; they also afford a starting point for thinking about issues of importance to them, like the nature of good and evil. And they simply like a good story about characters to whom they feel connected. When *The Witch Herself*, the third book of the first Witch trilogy, was published, the front flap indicated that it was the "conclusion." Immediately Naylor began receiving letters from readers such as that from a young girl who asked, "What is the meaning of this? Does this mean the end of Lynn and Mouse forever, or does this just mean the end of the three books? Please write more about witches and Lynn and Mouse. I love them dearly."[2] In response to the concerns of parents who threatened to withdraw their children from class if Naylor was visiting in fear of having them hear about witchcraft, Naylor's attitude is "I simply can't be bothered by that kind of criticism. If it decreases sales by half, then it decreases sales by half."[3]

Knowing that young adults have responded to her books positively means a great deal to Naylor; recognizing that she has touched the heart of a reader helps her maintain the energy needed to support efforts of librarians and teachers to keep her books on library shelves and in classrooms. *A String of Chances* came under fire from parents who thought that Evie should not have broken away from her father's faith. One father felt it would have been acceptable for Evie to question the religion of her family, but that Naylor should have shown her coming back into its fold at the end of the novel. This same father was upset by the "pagan" element in the book; he found Evie's attraction to the words of Chief Crowfoot threatening to his own children's belief structure. He wrote to the school librarian, the superintendent, and members of the school board, demanding that the book be taken off the shelf. Naylor wrote a letter of rebuttal, and a committee was formed to study the matter. But the father did not wait for their decision. He withdrew his children from the school, placed them in a private Christian school, and took the book from the library himself, refusing to give it back. Naylor sent the librarian another copy, and that was the end of the incident from her point of view.[4]

When *Shiloh* became the target of censors in a long, drawn-out battle over its appropriateness for classroom use, Naylor found herself heavily involved in its defense. In one school, a fourth-grade teacher taught *Shiloh* in the classroom, in part because of the book's selection as a Newbery winner and also because of the tremendous critical acclaim it received. But two parents complained to the school board about Judd Travers's use of "bad words." Since the school board seemingly had no policy in place for fielding parental protests, the superintendent instructed the teacher not to teach it in the classroom. The teacher objected, and a four-month fight began. Every time the issue was raised at a subsequent school board meeting, the report would surface on the front page of the town's newspaper. Naylor wrote letters of support to the teacher and the principal, and she composed another to the editor, describing what she hoped to accomplish in the book and her views on censorship in general. She says she wanted to "present a child from a loving, religious family who finds himself up against a vulgar, insensitive adult, and who, in the final analysis, must make a decision as to what he should do."[5] She found it curious that parents could object to Travers's language but not to his behavior—his ill treatment of his animals and his breaking of the law. She voiced her strong concern that taking *Shiloh* out of the hands of children would lead to attempts on other books until "all that remains are books so inoffensive that they are virtually useless in helping children face the real world."[6]

Eventually the teacher and the principal had to hire lawyers in order to defend their jobs, but the story had a happy ending. The school board ultimately failed to take any action against either the teacher or the book, partly because certain board members realized they were becoming a laughing stock in other states. The principal and teacher decided to continue to use *Shiloh* in the classroom.

Naylor notes that the energy involved in dealing with such situations is draining, but she also says she would travel anywhere anyone asked her to go in order to defend her work. As a child, her parents, in spite of their deep, traditional faith, encouraged her to read widely. As a parent herself, she never censored her sons' reading. Therefore it touches her heart to hear from a reader who has fallen in love with a book in spite of the efforts of others to take it away. For instance, Naylor recently received a large manila envelope containing the same teacher-dictated letter copied by every student in a fifth-grade class. They told her that because Judd uses foul language, they would not finish the book, would not read any book by Naylor, would not buy any more books from her publisher—and would tell their friends to follow suit. However, two boys had, in the tiniest handwriting, scrawled on the crease of their letters, so that their teacher would not see their words, "But we love your book anyway." It is those readers who inspire Naylor to continue doing whatever she can to enlarge their view of the world and to increase their awareness of their options as they stake out a place it.

On Getting Help as a Writer

In her efforts to write the best and truest books she can, Naylor enlists the aid of her family and her writer friends. She usually begins a book sitting in a brown tweed armchair positioned next to the fireplace in her comfortable Bethesda, Maryland, home. Drafting her story in longhand on a clipboard, she keeps a collection of three-ring notebooks nearby in which she jams all her notes, articles, and other information that may come in handy. When she has written through to the end of the novel, at least two complete drafts, she moves to her office, a paneled room lined with pictures of her family, where she word processes the book.[7]

Once the book leaves her computer, Naylor hands it over to her husband, Rex, a gentle-looking man with snow-white hair and a beard, whom she describes as a "harsh but thorough and fair critic," and the person most responsible for providing the atmosphere in which she can write. Naylor relies on Rex to give her feedback about the unity, character motivation, and clarity of the book, and she says he is also good about helping her find just the right word and correcting her spelling and grammar. When her sons were still living at home, they also helped her with her work.

One time she paid the younger to let her listen and observe as he and his friends played poker so that she could uncover the cadences of the conversation among a group of high-school buddies. As adolescents, both boys also read her books. Jeff, the older one, read because he was interested, and he sometimes did research for her, whereas Michael read, frankly, because he was paid to give her feedback. He was more interested in nonfiction. Now Jeff is married with children of his own. He and his wife Julie read Naylor's works to their daughters as they become ready for them.

Naylor also values her membership in the Children's Book Guild of Washington, D.C. This organization is made up of about 60 published writers and illustrators living in the Washington, D.C., area, as well as representatives from each school and public library system in the region. Whenever a member has a new book coming out, he or she introduces it at a monthly meeting and

West wall of Naylor's office: desk, typewriter, word processor (for drafts #3 and on); pictures of family grace the wall above the word processor.

A family gathering in Michigan, 1995. Back row from left: Nan Lee, Rex's daughter; Rex; Phyllis; Mike Naylor and fiancée, Jeanie Metz. Front row from left: daughter-in-law Julie, holding Tressa; Jeff; eldest granddaughter Sophia.

explains a bit about it. Naylor views her colleagues in the guild as friends rather than as competitors and values their support of each other in their new endeavors. She recalls that when the reviews of *Shiloh* first appeared, she was a bit discouraged. Although one reviewer gave it a star, another reviewer said it was not her best work—but she had felt it was the best children's book she had ever written. So, when she introduced the novel at a Guild meeting, she said, "No one will ever love this book as much as I do," and was delighted, several months later, to be proven wrong.

Naylor is also a part of a smaller critique group comprised of several other guild members, and these are the women with whom she has become close friends as well as colleagues. Marguerite Murray, author of *Like Seabirds Flying Home*, Joan Carris, who writes the "Aunt Morbelia" books, Peggy Thomson,

Phyllis Reynolds Naylor with granddaughter Sophia, "Sophie."

who won the *Boston Globe/Horn Book* award for *Auks, Rocks, and the Odd Dinosaur*, and Naylor have been reading and responding to each others' work for 12 years. They meet weekly, except during the summer months, on Monday nights, and they have recently welcomed back a former member, Larry Callen, author of *Pinch,* after his return to the area following many years in Louisiana. Naylor says she has noticed that when they first get together, they spend the first 20 minutes or so just talking about their week, "discouragements, illness, rejections, worries about children or spouses." They find they need to process all these emotional aspects of their lives so that they can later write about

Naylor's critique group. They have been meeting on Monday nights since 1981. In the home of Marguerite Murray are, from left to right, authors Peggy Thomson, Marguerite Murray, Phyllis Naylor, and Joan Carris.

these feelings with the clarity and perspective that comes with putting them into words within a caring, supportive community.[8]

In addition, Naylor corresponds with other authors whom she admires, including Marijane Meeker (M. E. Kerr), Lois Lowry, Carol Hurst, and Carol Farley. In these letters, she discusses everything from philosophical and religious questions to the mundane details of everyday life; this kind of writing, as well as meeting with her critique group, serves almost as psychotherapy, she says.

Given Naylor's attention to the craft of her writing and her delight in creating novels that present characters wrestling with serious issues, she has somewhat mixed feelings about writing series books. For instance, she began the "Bessledorf" books when her editor said the publisher wanted a mystery series comprised of books by various authors who would submit a book a year. Because the first components of the series were neither adequately promoted nor well received, that series died. But the editor enjoyed Naylor's contribution and asked for more, so Naylor has produced five of them over the past 10 years. She began the "Boys Against Girls" books because another publisher asked her to start a new series. Naylor argued to be allowed to appeal to both male and female readers by alternating the protagonist for each chapter, shifting from the boys' to the girls' perspective. Three books in the series have been published to date. She says of these series:

> These books are fun to do, and they make a nice change: I know there are lots of kids out there who enjoy them, particularly reluctant readers. I love that . . . so when I do them it's a nice, fun interlude. There's not much depth, but I allow myself to do that for the change of pace it gives me.

Naylor prefers to write about characters that take on a life of their own, as Alice did, and now as T. R. of the 1995 *Being Danny's Dog* has done. The sequel to *Shiloh—Shiloh Season* (1996)—is another case in which a character demanded that she write more about him. In general, she is opposed to the idea that a writer should try to cash in on a title that has been very popular, and her husband also was adamant that she not write a sequel to Marty's story. But one night as she was getting ready to leave the next morning by Amtrak to speak in Michigan, and as she was trying to sort out the scene of an adult novel that she hoped to start once she was on the train, the entire *Shiloh* sequel flashed into her mind. She reports that this was a "spooky" experience, that she has no idea what triggered her thought process, and she exclaimed, "No!" She added, "I'm *not* going to write a sequel to *Shiloh*." But sitting on the train the next day, facing her clipboard, the story kept eating at her, preventing her from working on the adult book, so she told herself she could write the first paragraph, just to get it out—and she had produced the whole first chapter before she knew it. As she wrote, she realized that her readers had posed some valid questions that may have subconsciously made her think about Marty's life after his showdown

The chair in Naylor's living room where she writes her first and second drafts in longhand (when she's not on Amtrak). Note rows of three-ring binders in which she keeps notes and clippings for books-to-be, each with title in masking tape on the spine. Above this shelf are her published books, for reference.

with Judd. Many students send letters to her about *Shiloh* noting that, although Marty rescued one dog, they wonder about the fate of Judd's other dogs. In the new book, Naylor says "the theme is no longer the moral question; it's about redemption, actually." It is Judd Travers who interests her now. Marty is still the same age, he is just dealing with the consequences of his actions in *Shiloh*. And there is a third—and final—book, Naylor says, to add to the list: *Saving Shiloh*, which deals with restitution. Can a

Naylor writing on Amtrak. She always has a bedroom for overnight travel, for privacy and quiet in which to think. She enjoys escaping, at least for a few days, the phone and mail. A few of her books have been written entirely on Amtrak, the first two drafts at least. One book is dedicated to Amtrak.

man of Judd's character ever be fully accepted back into the community?

The creation of vibrant, interesting, complex characters is Naylor's ultimate strength. The hallmarks of her craft—the juxtaposition of two personalities with very different world views, the use of detailed environmental descriptions to illustrate the inner state of an individual's emotions, the inclusion of much realistic, well-researched detail and attention to the cadences of dialogue and dialect—combine to create characters who touch the lives of their readers. With humor and the support of others, Alice, Nick, Beth, George, and their peers manage not only to survive whatever situation—of large or small consequence—is facing them, but also to demonstrate for their readers useful and comforting strategies for coping and moving forward with their lives.

Naylor says her most important advice to young adults is that they find ways to like themselves, and throughout her work she illustrates the difference between being comfortable with oneself and feeling a need to please the crowd. She notes that she did not feel this sense of comfort herself until she was close to 30, and she attributes the development of her ability to feel good about herself from the realization that she makes a contribution to the world and to others through her work.[9] She views her books somewhat similarly to the way a parent views a child, saying that sending a novel out into the world of readers resembles sending a child off to school knowing that once it leaves the house, it is on its own. The parent can no longer protect it: "You can't pave his way, and you have no control over what's happening in that outside world. You just have to hope, just like you do with your children, that you've instilled enough values, good judgment and common sense and self-esteem that it will survive and find its way."

Now a well-established, highly acclaimed writer, Naylor comments that her biggest problem is that she always has several books vying for her attention at once. She notes that just as she gets halfway through one story, another one comes to mind, begging for her to tell it. Naylor considers herself a lucky woman, blessed with a wonderful family and friends, a life rich in music and productive work, and a job that allows her to use her imagination in the service of her art.[10] In *How I Came to Be a Writer*, Naylor declares, "On my deathbed, I am sure, I will gasp, 'But I still have five more books to write!' ... I will go on writing, because an idea in the head is like a rock in the shoe; I just can't wait to get it out" (*How I Came*, 104). Naylor's readers are lucky to have the benefit of her artist's commitment, care, humor, and insight, and to have the company of the many and varied characters she has presented to the world.

Notes and References

Chapter 1

1. Phyllis Reynolds Naylor, *How I Came to Be a Writer* (New York: Macmillan, 1987, Aladdin Books edition): 7.
2. Phyllis Reynolds Naylor, publicity material from Atheneum, 1994.
3. Phyllis Reynolds Naylor, "More Than You Ever Wanted to Know About Me," unpublished; hereafter cited as "unpublished."
4. Unpublished.
5. Phyllis Reynolds Naylor, Letter to Lois Stover, August 15, 1995.
6. *Good Conversations! An Interview with Phyllis Reynolds Naylor.* Tim Podell Productions. Scarborough, NY, 1991; hereafter cited as *Good Conversations.*

Chapter 2

1. Caroline Ward, "The Agony of Alice," *School Library Journal* 32 (January 1986): 70.
2. "The Agony of Alice," *Booklist* 40 (October 1986): 52.
3. "Children's Choices for 1986," *The Reading Teacher* 40 (October 1986): 52 (38–55).
4. *Good Conversations.*
5. Hazel Rochman, "Alice in April," *Booklist* 89 (March 1989): 1223; hereafter cited as Rochman.
6. "Alice in Rapture, Sort of," *Language Arts* 66 (December 1989): 887.
7. Phyllis Reynolds Naylor, "Coming of Age with Alice" (Speech presented at the Adolescent Literature Assembly Workshop [ALAN], National Council of Teachers of English Fall Conference, Louisville, KY; 19 November 1992; hereafter cited as ALAN).
8. ALAN.

9.   David Elkind, All Grown Up and No Place to Go (Reading, Mass.: Addison-Wesley, 1984).
10.   ALAN.
11.   *Good Conversations.*
12.   ALAN.
13.   Phyllis Reynolds Naylor, "The Late Brennan Brothers," *Never Born a Hero* (Minneapolis: Augsburg Press, 1982): 22.
14.   Susan Hunter, "Alice In-Between," *School Library Journal* 40 (June 1994): 133–34.
15.   "Alice In-Between," *Horn Book* 70 (July/August 1994): 479.
16.   "Alice in Rapture, Sort Of" in "The USA Through Children's Books: 1988–1990," *Booklist* 86 (1 May 1990): 1716.
17.   Rochman.
18.   "All But Alice" in "Best Books of 1992," *School Library Journal* 38 (December 1992): 21.
19.   ALAN.

Chapter 3

1.   ALAN.
2.   "Footprints at the Window: The York Trilogy, Book III," *Booklist* 78 (15 October 1981): 309.
3.   Chuck Schact, "Shadows on the Wall," *School Library Journal* 27 (January 1981): 71–72.
4.   "Faces in the Water: The York Trilogy, Book II," *Horn Book* 57 (August 1981): 435.
5.   "Shadows on the Wall," *Publishers Weekly* 218 (5 December 1980): 52.
6.   "Faces in the Water; The York Trilogy, Book II," *Booklist* 77 (1 May 1981): 1109.
7.   "The Solomon System," *Horn Book* 59 (October 1983): 585.
8.   Gayle Berge, "The Solomon System," *School Library Journal* 30 (October 1983): 161.
9.   "The Keeper," *Booklist* 82 (1 April 1986): 1144.
10.   Pat Scales, "More Books to Teach," *Booklist* 86 (1 March 1990): 1355; Libby White, "The Keeper," *School Library Journal* 32 (May 1986): 107.

Chapter 4

1.   Alice Casey, "Ice," *School Library Journal* 41 (October 1995): 169; hereafter cited as Casey.
2.   Roger Sutton, "A String of Chances," *School Library Journal* 29 (September 1982): 142.

3. Unpublished.
4. Unpublished.
5. Unpublished.
6. Letter to Stover, from Naylor, August 15, 1995.
7. "Notable Children's Trade Books in the Field of Social Studies," *Social Education* 47 (April 1983): 240–52 (p. 251).
8. Steve Matthews, "The Year of the Gopher," *School Library Journal* 33 (May 1987): 116.
9. "The Year of the Gopher," *Booklist* 83 (1 March 1981): 1008.
10. Phyllis Reynolds Naylor, "Starting Over," in *Change in the Wind* (Minneapolis: Augsburg Press, 1979), 57–61.
11. Unpublished.
12. Unpublished.
13. Pat Klatka, "Send No Blessings," *School Library Journal* 36 (October 1990): 143; hereafter cited as Klatka.
14. Klatka.
15. Hazel Rochman, "Send No Blessings," *Booklist* 87 (1 November 1990): 518.
16. "Best Books on Young Adults in 1991," *Booklist* 87 (15 March 1991): 1478.

Chapter 5

1. Ruth M. Stein, "Book ReMarks: A Personal View of Current Juvenile Literature," *Language Arts* 53 (September 1976): 701.
2. Lillian N. Gerhardt, "Walking through the Dark," *School Library Journal* 22 (April 1976): 93.
3. "Walking through the Dark," *Horn Book* 52 (June 1976): 295.
4. Joanne S. Gillespie, "Reliving the Depression: Integrating English and Social Studies," *English Journal* 79 (October 1990): 64–69 (p. 67).
5. Letter to Stover, August 15, 1995.
6. "Night Cry," *Horn Book* 60 (June 1984): 331.
7. Maria Salvadore, "Night Cry," *School Library Journal* 30 (April 1984): 126.
8. Bryna J. Fireside, "Young Adult Books: A Response to 'Members of the Last Generation,' " *Horn Book* 62 (January/February 1986): 89–92 (p. 91).
9. Nancy P. Reeder, "The Dark of the Tunnel," *School Library Journal* 31 (May 1985): 103.
10. Judy Beekman, "Junior Books Too Good to Miss," *English Journal* 63 (March 1974): 104–6 (105).
11. Genevieve Stuttaford, ed., "Forecasts—*Unexpected Pleasures*," *Publishers Weekly* 230 (25 July 1986): 173.

12. Letter to Stover, August 15, 1995.
13. Kay Bonetti, "An Interview with Phyllis Reynolds Naylor" (American Audio Prose Library 1987); hereafter cited as Bonetti.
14. Bonetti.
15. Bonetti.
16. Bonetti.

Chapter 6

1. Bonetti.
2. Bonetti.
3. Bonetti.
4. Bonetti.
5. Bonetti.
6. Jean Karl, Letter to Lois Stover, May 21, 1995.
7. Casey.
8. Bonetti.
9. Phyllis Reynolds Naylor, "The Writing of *Shiloh*," *The Reading Teacher* 46 (September 1992): 10–12 (10); hereafter cited as "The Writing of *Shiloh*,"
10. "The Writing of *Shiloh*," 11.
11. "The Writing of *Shiloh*," 11.
12. "The Writing of *Shiloh*," 12.

Chapter 7

1. Bonetti.
2. Unpublished.
3. Bonetti.
4. Bonetti.
5. Phyllis Reynolds Naylor, "Letter to the Editor," *The News Journal*, (Columbia, Louisiana), February 4, 1994; hereafter cited as letter to the editor.
6. Letter to the editor.
7. *Good Conversations*.
8. Letter to Stover.
9. Bonetti.
10. Donna Olendorf, ed., *Something about the Author, Vol. 66*. (Detroit: Gale Research, 1991), 170–77.

Selected Bibliography

Primary Sources

Young Adult Novels

To Shake a Shadow. Nashville: Abingdon Press, 1967.
When Rivers Meet. New York: Friendship Press, 1968.
Making It Happen. Chicago: Follett, 1970.
No Easy Circle. Chicago: Follett, 1972.
Walking through the Dark. New York: Atheneum, 1976.
Shadows on the Wall (York Trilogy, Pt. I). New York: Atheneum, 1980.
Faces in the Water (York Trilogy, Pt. II). New York: Atheneum, 1981.
Footprints at the Window (York Trilogy, Pt. III). New York: Atheneum, 1981.
A String of Chances. New York: Atheneum, 1982.
The Solomon System. New York: Atheneum, 1983.
Night Cry. New York: Atheneum, New York, 1984.
The Dark of the Tunnel. New York: Atheneum, 1985.
The Keeper. New York: Atheneum, 1986.
The Year of the Gopher. New York: Atheneum, 1987.
Send No Blessings. New York: Atheneum, 1990.
Ice. New York: Atheneum, 1995.

Young Adult Novels: The "Alice" Series

The Agony of Alice. New York: Atheneum, 1985.
Alice in Rapture, Sort Of. New York: Atheneum, 1989.
Reluctantly Alice. New York: Atheneum, New York, 1991.
All But Alice. New York: Atheneum, 1992.
Alice in April. New York; Atheneum, 1993.
Alice In-Between. New York: Atheneum, 1994.
Alice the Brave. New York: Atheneum, 1995.
Alice in Lace. New York: Atheneum, 1996.

Short Story Collections

The Galloping Goat and Other Stories. Nashville, Tenn.: Abingdon Press, 1965.
Grasshoppers in the Soup. Philadelphia: Fortress Press, 1965.
Knee Deep in Ice Cream. Philadelphia: Fortress Press, 1967.
Dark Side of the Moon. Philadelphia: Fortress Press, 1969.
The Private I. Philadelphia: Fortress Press, 1969.
Ships in the Night. Philadelphia: Fortress Press, 1970.
A Change in the Wind. Minneapolis: Augsburg Press, 1979.
Never Born a Hero. Minneapolis: Augsburg Press, 1982.
A Triangle Has Four Sides. Minneapolis: Augsburg Press, 1984.

Children's Picture Books

Jennifer Jean, Cross-Eyed Queen. Minneapolis: Lerner, 1978.
The New Schoolmaster. Morristown, NJ: Silver Burdett, 1967.
A New Year's Surprise. Morristown, N.J.: Silver Burdett, 1967.
Meet Murdock. Chicago: Follett, 1969.
The Boy with the Helium Head. New York: Atheneum, 1982.
Old Sadie and the Christmas Bear. New York: Atheneum, 1984.
The Baby, the Bed, and the Rose. New York: Clarion Press, 1987.
Keeping a Christmas Secret. New York: Atheneum, 1989.
King of the Playground. New York: Atheneum, 1991.
Duck's Disappearing. New York: Atheneum, 1997.
I Can't Take You Anywhere. New York: Atheneum, 1997.

Children's Novels

What the Gulls Were Singing. Chicago: Follett, 1967.
To Make a Wee Moon. Chicago: Follett, 1969.
Wrestle the Mountain. Chicago: Follett, 1971.
To Walk the Sky Path. Chicago: Follett, 1973.
How Lazy Can You Get? New York: Atheneum, 1979.
Eddie, Incorporated. New York: Atheneum, 1980.
All Because I'm Older. New York: Atheneum, 1981.
Beetles, Lightly Toasted. New York: Atheneum, 1987.
Maudie in the Middle. New York: Atheneum, 1988. (Coauthored with Lura Schield Reynolds, Naylor's mother.)
One of the Third Grade Thonkers. New York: Atheneum, 1988.
Shiloh. New York: Atheneum, 1991.
Josie's Troubles. New York: Atheneum, 1992.
The Grand Escape. New York: Atheneum, 1993.
The Boys Start the War. New York: Delacorte, 1993.
The Girls Get Even. New York: Delacorte, 1993.

Boys Against Girls. New York: Delacorte, 1994.
The Fear Place. New York: Atheneum, 1994.
Being Danny's Dog. New York: Atheneum, 1995.
Shiloh Season. New York: Atheneum, 1996.

Children's Novels: The "Witch" Series

Witch's Sister. New York: Atheneum, 1975.
Witch Water. New York: Atheneum, 1977.
The Witch Herself. New York: Atheneum, 1978.
The Witch's Eye. New York: Delacorte, 1990.
Witch Weed. New York: Delacorte, 1991.
The Witch Returns. New York: Delacorte, 1992.

Children's Novels: The "Bessledorf" Mystery Series

The Mad Gasser of Bessledorf Street. New York: Atheneum, 1983.
The Bodies in the Bessledorf Hotel. New York: Atheneum, 1986.
Bernie and the Bessledorf Ghost. New York: Atheneum, 1990.
The Face in the Bessledorf Funeral Parlor. New York: Atheneum, 1993.
The Bomb in the Bessledorf Bus Depot. New York: Atheneum, 1997.

Nonfiction for Children and Young Adults

How to Find Your Wonderful Someone. Philadelphia: Fortress Press, 1972.
An Amish Family. Chicago: J. Phillip O'Hara Publishing Co., 1974.
Getting Along in Your Family. Nashville: Abingdon, 1976.
How I Came to Be a Writer. New York: Atheneum, 1978.
Getting Along with Your Friends. Nashville: Abingdon, 1979.
Getting Along with Your Teachers. Nashville: Abingdon, 1981.

Adult Fiction and Nonfiction

Crazy Love: An Autobiographical Account of Marriage and Madness. New York: Morrow, 1977.
In Small Doses. New York: Atheneum, 1979.
Revelations. New York: St. Martin's Press, 1979.
Unexpected Pleasures. New York: Putnam, 1986.
The Craft of Writing the Novel. Boston: The Writer, Inc., 1989.

Works in Progress

Strawberries (picture book)
The Treasure of Bessledorf Hill (children's novel)
Carrying On (adult novel)
Danny's Desert Rats (children's novel)

Faith, Hope, and Ivy June (children's novel)
Carlotta's Kittens (children's novel)
The Healing of Texas Jake (children's novel)
Sang Spell (YA novel)
Outrageously Alice (YA novel)
The Grooming of Alice (YA novel)
Smoke Water (children's novel)
Patrick's Picnic (picture book)
Achingly Alice (YA novel)
Saving Shiloh (children's novel)

Secondary Sources

Articles

Gallo, Donald R. (ed.). "Phyllis Reynolds Naylor." *Speaking for Ourselves, Too.* Urbana, Ill.: National Council of Teachers of English, 1993. 146–49

Kovacs, Deborah, and James Preller. "Phyllis Reynolds Naylor." *Meet the Authors and Illustrators.* Vol. 2. New York: Scholastic Professional Books, 1993. 120–21.

Naylor, Phyllis Reynolds. "The Writing of Shiloh." *The Reading Teacher* 46 (September 1992): 10–12.

Olendorf, Donna (ed.). "Phyllis Reynolds Naylor." *Something about the Author.* Vol. 66. Detroit: Gale Publishing, 1991. 170–77.

Interviews

Bonetti, Kay. Interview with Phyllis Reynolds Naylor. Central Missouri State University, American Prose Library, 1987.

Graham, Joyce. "An Interview with Phyllis Reynolds Naylor." *Journal of Youth Services in Libraries* 6 (Summer 1993): 392–98.

Stover, Lois. Interview with Phyllis Reynolds Naylor. Columbia, Md. (June 1995). Unpublished.

Speeches

Phyllis Reynolds Naylor. "Coming of Age with Alice." Speech given at Adolescent Literature Assembly Workshop during the National Council of Teachers of English Fall Conference, Louisville, KY, November 19, 1992.

Phyllis Reynolds Naylor. "More Than You Ever Wanted to Know About Me." Unpublished.

Films

Good Conversation! An Interview with Phyllis Reynolds Naylor. Tim Podell Productions, Scarborough, NY, 1991.
My Dad Can't Be Crazy . . . Can He? Adapted from the book *The Keeper.* American Broadcast Company's *After-School Special* series. Aired 14 September 1989.

Book Reviews (Selected)

THE AGONY OF ALICE
"Children's Choices for 1986." *The Reading Teacher* 40 (October 1986): 38–55.
Ward, Caroline. *School Library Journal* 32 (January 1986): 70.

ALICE IN APRIL
Rochman, Hazel. *Booklist* 89 (March 1989): 1223.

ALICE IN-BETWEEN
Hunter, Susan. *School Library Journal* 40 (June 1994): 133–34.

ALICE IN RAPTURE, SORT OF
Language Arts 66 (December 1989): 887.
"The U. S. A. Through Children's Books: 1988–1990." *Booklist* 86 (1 May 1990): 1716.

ALL BUT ALICE
"Best Books of 1992." *School Library Journal* 38 (December 1992): 21.

THE DARK OF THE TUNNEL
Fireside, Bryna J. "Young Adult Books: A Response to 'Members of the Last Generation.'" *Horn Book* 62 (January/February 1986): 89–92.
Reeder, Nancy. *School Library Journal* 31 (May 1985): 103.

FOOTPRINTS AT THE WINDOW
Booklist 78 (October 1981): 309.

FACES IN THE WATER
Booklist 77 (1 May 1981): 1109.

ICE
Casey, Alice. *School Library Journal* 41 (October 1995): 169.

THE KEEPER
Booklist 82 (1 April 1986): 1144.
Scales, Pat. "More Books to Teach." *Booklist* 86 (1 March 1990): 1344.
White, Libby. *School Library Journal* 32 (May 1986): 107.

NIGHT CRY
Horn Book 60 (June 1984): 331.

Salvadore, Maria. *School Library Journal* 30 (April 1984): 126.

NO EASY CIRCLE
Beekman, Judy. "Junior Books Too Good to Miss." *English Journal* 63 (March 1974): 104–6.

SEND NO BLESSINGS
"Best Books for Young Adults." *Booklist* 87 (15 March 1991): 1478.
Klatka, Pat. *School Library Journal* 36 (October 1990): 143.
Rochman, Hazel. *Booklist* 87 (1 November 1990): 518.

SHADOWS ON THE WALL
Schact, Chuck. *School Library Journal* 27 (January 1981): 71–72.

THE SOLOMON SYSTEM
Berge, Gayle. *School Library Journal* 30 (October 1983): 161.
Horn Book 59 (October 1983): 585.

A STRING OF CHANCES
"Notable Children's Trade Books in the Field of Social Studies." *Social Education* 47 (April 1983): 240–52.
Sutton, Roger. *School Library Journal* 29 (September 1982): 142.

UNEXPECTED PLEASURES
Stuttaford, Genevieve (ed.). "Forecasts—Unexpected Pleasures." *Publishers Weekly* 250 (25 July 1986): 173.

WALKING THROUGH THE DARK
Gerhardt, Lillian N. *School Library Journal* 22 (April 1976): 93.
Gillespie, Joanne S. "Reliving the Depression: Integrating English and Social Studies." *English Journal* 79 (October 1990): 64–69.
Horn Book 51 (June 1976): 295.
Stein, Ruth. "Book ReMarks: A Personal View of Current Juvenile Literature." *Language Arts* 53 (September 1976): 701.

THE YEAR OF THE GOPHER
Booklist 83 (1 March 1987): 1008.
Matthew, Steve. *School Library Journal* 33 (May 1987): 116.

Index

The Author

Lois Thomas Stover is the chair of the Educational Studies Department at St. Mary's College of Maryland where she supervises student teachers and teaches courses in pedagogy, educational psychology, literacy, and foundations of education. A former middle school teacher of English and drama, she edited the *English Journal's* Young Adult Literature column for two years, has served as the editor of *Books for You,* the National Council of Teachers of English's booklist for senior high students, and has written numerous chapters and articles for various publications, such as *The ALAN Review,* and *Adolescent Literature as a Complement to the Classics.*

The Editor

Patricia J. Campbell is an author and critic specializing in books for young adults. She has taught adolescent literature at UCLA and is the former Assistant Coordinator of Young Adult Services for the Los Angeles Public Library. Her literary criticism has been published in the *New York Times Book Review* and many other journals. From 1978 to 1988 her column "The YA Perplex," a monthly review of young adult books, appeared in the *Wilson Library Bulletin*. She now writes a column on controversial issues in adolescent literature for *Horn Book* magazine. Campbell is the author of five books, among them *Presenting Robert Cormier,* the first volume in the Twayne Young Adult Author Series. In 1989 she was the recipient of the American Library Association Grolier Award for distinguished achievement with young people and books. A native of Los Angeles, Campbell now lives on an avocado ranch near San Diego, where she and her husband, David Shore, write and publish books on overseas motor home travel.